The Humility Factor

Gus,
Thanks for the friendship.
John

The Humility Factor

HEALTHY CHURCHES ARE LED BY HUMBLE PASTORS

Dr. John Plastow

**Forewords by
Pastor N. Graham Standish
Pastor Arron Chambers**

Edited by Karen Plastow

© 2017 Dr. John Plastow
All rights reserved.

ISBN: 1979588228
ISBN 13: 9781979588225
Library of Congress Control Number: 2017917520
CreateSpace Independent Publishing Platform
North Charleston, South Carolina

Endorsements for *The Humility Factor*

Don't read this book if you're hoping to feel really proud of your humility level! Humility is hard because it actually requires a lot from us, not the least of which are both self-awareness and self-denial. After reading and reflecting on *The Humility Factor*, I was reminded of the old saying, *"it's not about thinking less of yourself, but rather thinking about yourself less."*

John Plastow shares a helpful and insightful model on assessing humility, and in the process also includes candid illustrations of his own failures to be humble, inspiring his readers to consider their own. All of us should want to pursue humility because, according to Jesus, humility is the acid test of spiritual leadership. *"For all those who exalt themselves will be humbled, and those who humble themselves will be exalted."* (Luke 14:11 NIV)

Humility often appears too little and too late among strong leaders. We love to take the lead and to take charge. We speak up and speak often. We enjoy being recognized and being rewarded. We compare ourselves with ourselves and only rarely compare ourselves with Christ, the One who humbled Himself by serving us and even dying for us. I recommend that you read this book not primarily to evaluate "the humility factor" in someone else, but in yourself!

Pastor Alan Ahlgrim
Center for Church Leadership

I have had a front row seat for much of the personal journey that is described in John Plastow's *The Humility Factor*. What I didn't fully have, up until now, was an intimate insight into the thinking and the metamorphosis that was taking place within the heart of a true servant of God. This book is destined to be a landmark, not only

in the church leadership literature, but also in the general leadership literature at large. It weaves poignant narratives into the fabric of powerful teaching on the desperate need for humble servant leaders in today and tomorrow's church. Church leadership is hard; having a humble heart doing it is essential. John Plastow has effectively articulated the need for and the characteristics of a humble church leader. While written for a church audience, it has far reaching implications that can, and should, be applied to business, education, and non-profit leaders. It will be added to the essential reading list that I recommend to any up-and-coming aspiring leader. We all need the lessons presented in this book!
> **Douglas M. DeWitt, Ph.D.**
> **Chair: Department of Education Leadership and Graduate Studies**
> **Salisbury University**

"Fantastic! What a convergent work! I appreciate the style and format John uses to present the model he has created. He takes time to look at the model from multiple leadership styles, which gives *The Humility Factor* a thorough presentation and helps the reader forecast the application. . . What a tremendous work. It has the capacity to influence leadership thinking, language and behavior much the way Goleman has influenced thinking and the use of Emotional Intelligence. . . John's work demonstrates a convergence of critical thinking, biblical integration, and a product with the capacity to influence and guide Christian Leaders who are Changing the World."
> **Diane M. Wiater, PhD**
> **Adjunct Professor**
> **Regent University, School of Business & Leadership**

Therefore if you have any encouragement from being united with Christ, if any comfort from his love, if any common sharing in the

Spirit, if any tenderness and compassion, then make my joy complete by being like-minded, having the same love, being one in spirit and of one mind. Do nothing out of selfish ambition or vain conceit. Rather, in humility value others above yourselves, not looking to your own interests but each of you to the interests of the others. In your relationships with one another, have the same mindset as Christ Jesus: Who, being in very nature[a] God, did not consider equality with God something to be used to his own advantage; rather, he made himself nothing by taking the very nature[b] of a servant, being made in human likeness. And being found in appearance as a man, he humbled himself by becoming obedient to death—even death on a cross! Therefore God exalted him to the highest place and gave him the name that is above every name, that at the name of Jesus every knee should bow, in heaven and on earth and under the earth, and every tongue acknowledge that Jesus Christ is Lord, to the glory of God the Father (Philippians 2: 1-11).

When you read this thought-provoking, heart-challenging, life-changing message from Dr. John Plastow, you will look at Philippians 2 in a whole new light. It was Jesus who exemplified the importance of a life of humility, surrender, and prayer. The lifelong struggle for those who are looked up to is in remembering we do not seek the spotlight; that was assigned from the foundation of the world.

John writes in a warm and persuasive way illustrating things that should have seemed obvious. I think it would do readers well to bring a couple highlighter pens to this endeavor. There are so many examples, stories, and personal experiences woven though these pages.

I encourage you to pray for illumination which will lead to inspiration. The humility factor consists of seven attributes of humility modeled by Jesus Christ in His actions and words. Note that these are not a list to be chosen from at the leader's discretion, but rather, all are necessary for the humility factor to be evident.

Blessing to you John, I intend to quote you a lot - now off to the store to buy a few more highlighter pens.
> **Randy Vader**
> **Founder and CEO**
> **PraiseGathering Music Group**

I have known John Plastow for over 30 years and have always known him to be energetic, passionate, driven and cutting-edge, with a huge desire to reach people for Christ through the arts! John has a strong gift of leadership, and to see his embracing of "Servant Leadership" in *The Humility Factor* is very rewarding. He leaves no stone unturned in his in-depth study on the subject in this great book! The concept of compassion, sacrificial service, brokenness and forgiveness seems to be missing from many of today's leaders. John calls us all back to Christ's example to embrace Philippians 2:3 and 'In humility, value others above ourselves.

John's honesty and transparency draw us all to be leaders of integrity and honor with a huge dose of humility!
   Thank you, John Plastow, for reminding us to pursue the likeness of Christ and walk in humility as we lead our people.
> **Dr. Phil Barfoot**
> **CEO / President**
> **Celebration Concert Tours International / CCT Music**
> **Franklin, TN**

In a day of entitlement, when narcissism is confused with strength of leadership and is so readily accepted, even in the church, this call to humility and servant leadership is urgently

needed. When the leader develops humble intelligence, everyone wins and everything in the organization improves. Thank you, John Plastow, for your insights in this excellent, helpful and transparent book.
Pastor Paul Gilbert
Grace Fellowship Church
Buffalo, Wyoming

In his book The Humility Factor, Dr. John Plastow shines a timely light on a subject that is vital to every member of the modern church: humble leadership. More often than we'd like to admit, there's a sense in today's church that power grabs and trendy programs are the norm, but churches longing to see a deepening of faith in their members and new seekers coming to Christ will take a hard look at Plastow's research. The great need for pastors and ministry teams to lead with humility will resonate with any Christ-follower who is invested in stopping the decline of the American church.
Kimberly Messer, Executive Director of
Communications, Challenge Charter Schools
Writer/Creative Consultant

John Plastow clearly understands that the most important decision any church can make is to decide who gets asked to lead the pastoral team. In The Humility Factor, Plastow equips church leaders with a tool to measure what has heretofore been subjective at best--a servant's heart. This method rescues and re-centers the hiring process away from the ego-driven mega personality and grounds it in scriptural principle. I'd recommend this book to any group that is considering the hire of a servant leader.
Dr. Brett Andrews, Dean
School of Business
Newman University

DR. JOHN PLASTOW

This book was just the breath of fresh air I needed in my leadership journey. Dr. Plastow doesn't ignore the reality of the need for great leadership in the church. Far from it. What he **does** do is address the tension that exists between being the leader your church wants and the servant/shepherd that your church needs. This is a tension that most pastors either ignore or try to solve, but that simply needs to be managed with humility. I would recommend this book to anyone in ministry who is brave enough to wrestle with that tension.
    Pastor Phill Tague
    Lead Pastor
    The Ransom Church
    Sioux Falls, South Dakota

Your book with its introduction of *humble intelligence* has significant potential to be viewed as a pivot concept in the field of leadership. It serves as an important intervention tool for church boards and lay leaders to hire and develop pastors who will lead with humility. *The Humility Factor* model outlines a framework model to help pastors "to become more effective because of their heightened focus on meeting the needs of people over seeking their own benefit; their leadership inspires others to join the team and pursue God-sized initiatives; and the church becomes a place to which the community looks when something important needs to get done, and is considered with high respect and regard." The entire premise is framed around the aspiration to attain *humble intelligence* by modeling the leadership of Jesus.
    Dr. Virginia Richardson, BCC
    Founder & CEO, Foresight Center
    Professor of Strategic Leadership & Foresight
    Regent University, School of Business & Leadership

If true Christ-like leadership and real servant leadership is what you desire or your church is looking for in its next pastor or leader, *The Humility Factor* is a must read. In these pages, Dr. John Plastow explores and shines the light on the seven attributes that make up a humble servant. These are not platitudes or impersonal directives. The points that John makes are harvested from his own life and ministry experience. This book is good for pastors as well as board members and laymen of all walks. As I read these pages, I was automatically forced to do a personal assessment. Warning: reading this book will cause you to do the same.

George Baldwin, Producer, Publisher and Creative Consultant

Dedication

This book is dedicated to my wife and life partner, Karen, who has patiently walked with me every step of my humility journey. I often refer to her as a "saint" because living with me has been an ongoing challenge due to the many lessons God needed to teach me and is still teaching me. It's amazing to me that she has been willing to put up with it all! Our life journey has been filled with terrific experiences, both difficult and exhilarating, and my greatest blessing has been her willingness to do whatever task was needed, listen to me rant, and persevere through the challenges of a life of ministry. She is an excellent example of a humble servant. The doctoral process and the project which this book represents was made possible because of her support, love, and editing! Thank you!

I also dedicate this book to my three extraordinary children who are all pursuing a life of passion and purpose that will honor God and make a difference in this world. I am excited to see what God does in them and through them as they serve others in the humble way of Jesus.

To Karen, John II, Melody, and Heather…I love you.

Acknowledgements

I would like to thank:

My wife, Karen, and children, John II, Melody, and Heather
Kay Davis and Ed Plastow for your support in encouraging me to pursue my doctorate
The thousands who have given me the pleasure to serve them and lead them in the local church
The countless ministry leaders with whom I have served through the years
Maryellen Landers - forever friends
Doug DeWitt – I have been…

I would also like to thank the following pastors who have directly contributed to this book:

Arron Chambers, Young Chin Cho, Steven Grant, Greg Hafeman, Paul Hoffman, Steve Jacobsen,
Leon Johnson, John Knutson, David McNeff, Wes Moore, David Sather, Scott Slayback,
Nathan Soule-Hill, Graham Standish, Jack Stapleton, Thomas Thompson, Jim Tracey,

Michael Walter, and the pastor of First United Methodist Church of Loveland, CO, who desired to remain unnamed.

I would especially like to thank:

- Dr. Virginia Richardson for her guidance as the chair of my final doctoral project
- Dr. Kathleen Patterson, Dr. Doris Gomez, and Dr. Bruce Winston for their encouragement throughout the doctoral program
- Dr. Diane M. Wiater and Dr. Gary Oster for their over-the-top academic investment in me, their care and friendship, and for the opportunities they have provided
- And to the many other professors who helped me to complete this program

Table of Contents

Acknowledgements ······················ xv

Foreword by Pastor N. Graham Standish ······ xxi

Foreword by Pastor Arron Chambers ········ xxvii

Preface: Promptings ····················· xxxi

Chapter 1 Healthy Churches are Led by Humble Pastors ··· 1

    Introduction ························· 1

    Successful, Effective, Healthy ··············· 7

    Churches Need Strong Leaders, but… ········ 8

    Humility Toward God ···················· 9

    Jesus: Humble Servant ·················· 11

What's the Point? What's at Stake? What's
Missing? · 13

What is the Humility Factor? · · · · · · · · · · · · · · · 25

The Humility Factor Model · · · · · · · · · · · · · · · · 27

Chapter 2 The Journey to Humility · 35

My Personal Humility Journey and Lessons
Learned (so far) · 35

Chapter 3 Here's How the Humility Factor Works · · · · · · · · 49

Input from Pastor Graham Standish · · · · · · · · · · 50

What is Humility? What Does it Look Like?
How Did Jesus Model it? · · · · · · · · · · · · · · · · · 55

Seven Signs of the Humility Factor · · · · · · · · · · 59

Compassion · 61

Sacrificial Service · 69

Openness · 74

Brokenness · 81

Self-Awareness · 86

Forgiveness · 93

Gratitude · 98

Chapter 4 So Many Pastoral Leaders to Choose From! · · 103

Pastoral Leadership Styles · · · · · · · · · · · · · · · 103

Help Wanted: The Job Description
of a Pastor · 107

Survey Data Results and Discovery · · · · · · · · · 111

The Pastoral Leadership Buffet · · · · · · · · · · · · 121

Application of Humble Intelligence
to Leadership Styles · · · · · · · · · · · · · · · · · · · 169

Chapter 5 It's Time to Hire a New Pastor! · · · · · · · · · · · · · 177

How to Hire a Pastor with the Humility
Factor in Mind · 177

The Humility Factor Assessment Instrument · · 185

Chapter 6 Humility Matters · 189

So What? Who Cares? What's at Stake? · · · · 189

7 Ways How <u>Not</u> to be a Pastor of Humble
Intelligence · 195

An Unparalleled Example ················ 205

Final Thoughts from a Work in Progress ····· 208

Endnotes ······························· 211

About the Author ························ 243

Foreword by Pastor N. Graham Standish

A few months ago I had a conversation with one of those "salt of the earth" people who seem unsophisticated on the outside, but have a homespun wisdom that can take complex ideas and make them simple. We chatted about a wide range of topics. Many of his responses were punctuated by shrugs, smiles, and a wrinkled nose. Eventually we moved to the problem of modern American politics. He quickly summarized all of the issues with a smile, saying, "We've got a bumper crop of arrogance, and too many people are getting fat on it."

That pretty much sums up the North American malaise. Ironically and sadly our modern feasting on arrogance is in direct contrast to the experience of the early Christians. In his wonderful book, *The Patient Ferment of the Early Church*, historian Alan Kreider talks about the personal qualities cherished by Christians that led the early church to grow exponentially over the first 250 years of Christianity.

The church grew rapidly during a time when being a Christian was dangerous. The Roman Empire's responses to the church ranged from constant criticism and denigration to outright oppression, torture, imprisonment, and grisly execution. Still the church grew exponentially, even if a bit unevenly, throughout the empire. Why would it grow when it was so dangerous to be a Christian? Kreider explains,

> The early Christians had a perspective that they called 'patience.' They believed that God was in charge of events; they knew they were not... Christian leaders didn't think or write about how to systematize the spread of Christianity; they were not concerned to cover the world evenly with evangelistic efforts. Instead the Christians concentrated on developing practices that contributed to a habitus that characterized both individual Christians and Christian communities. They believed that when the habitus was healthy, the churches would grow.[i]

Early church pastors and leaders saw the Great Commission (Matthew 28:16-20) differently from modern Christians. Today we often see it as the process of making rational Christian arguments that convince people that Christ is the way. The early church didn't see the commission in this way. They saw the Great Commission as God's responsibility. Their responsibility, which Kreider called their "habitus," or way of living, was "patience." Kreider was right, but there was more to it than mere patience. Patience is something of a subset of the greater Christian virtue of humility, the value of which has been neglected in the modern Christian church.

Early church leaders had a sense of humility that allowed them to be patient. Much like Jesus' parable of the sower, they saw their responsibility as humbly spreading seeds of the Gospel that the Spirit would then nurture and cultivate. They were to live the Gospel and demonstrate it in their lives in

[i] Kreider, Alan. *The Patient Ferment of the Early Church: The Improbable rise of Christianity in the Roman Empire*, Kindle Edition (Baker Academic: Grand Rapids, MI, 2016), location 2227.

a way that St. Francis articulated 1000 years later when he said, "Preach the Gospel always, and when necessary use words." Their evangelism was the example of their lives, and people wanted to become like them because they weren't like others in the Roman Empire.

They were scrupulously honest in business dealings, and often forgave debts. They took in those who were struggling and suffering. They reached out to those down on their luck. They were unfailingly pleasant to each other and to outsiders. When unfairly imprisoned, beaten, made sport of in local coliseums, or executed, more often than not they visibly cared for each other in the process. They attracted converts because people wanted their kinds of lives. They were patient with everything, but even more, they were humble.

Rarely does modern Christianity offer humility as the way. We are much more used to seeing Christian leaders appearing on television or in public with prophetic finger-wagging, anguished outrage, or apoplectic edicts, all while proclaiming political allegiances… and sometimes, when their lives implode, offering anguished apologies.

Is it any wonder that people are leaving Christianity, or at least leaving the church? At the same time, is it any wonder that Pope Francis has become such a popular figure among non-Catholics, especially those who've left the church? The quality I hear so many apply to him is that he's humble, and that they are so glad to finally see a humble Christian. Reflect on this for a moment: they are glad to see a *humble* Christian.

What's happened that we've lost our collective humility? I believe it's the Americanization of Christianity. We live in a culture of "look-at-me." From athletes to celebrities to politicians to pundits, from Facebook to Instagram to YouTube, people want to be noticed. They want to be praised. They want to be important. Humility's a problem because it seems so… unimportant.

The real problem of modern life is that we confuse humility with weakness, with being pushed around and victimized. Humility isn't weakness. It actually entails tremendous strength. As the cherished Quaker spiritual writer, Thomas Kelly, says,

> Humility does not rest, in the final count, upon bafflement and discouragement and self-disgust at our shabby lives, a brow-beaten, dog-slinking attitude. It rests upon the disclosure of the consummate wonder of God, upon finding that only God counts, that all our own self-originated intentions are works of straw. And so in lowly humility we must stick close to the Root and count our own powers as nothing except that they are enslaved in His power.[ii]

It takes real strength to stick close to the Root and to realize that only God counts. It takes real strength to humbly and patiently say to someone, "I won't follow you because I would lose God in the process. So, I'll endure whatever you want to do to me, but I'm going to follow what God wants."

[ii] Thomas R. Kelly, *A Testament of Devotion* (San Francisco: HarperSanFrancisco, 1992)

To have this kind of humility, the kind that John Plastow explores here in his work, *The Humility Factor*, is to demonstrate real courage. It takes courage to base our work on qualities such as compassion, sacrificial service, openness, brokenness, self-awareness, forgiveness, and gratitude. Take a little time of honest reflection and think about our country's leaders. Compare their lives to the qualities on this checklist. How many of these qualities can you check off as you describe their qualities? Now reflect on the people you admire most in life—whether that's a parent, a friend, a public figure, or a figure of history. How many of these qualities can you check off when looking at their lives?

As Christian leaders, we are called to a different standard, and the standard, as John Plastow points out, begins with humility. Yet humility is so hard for so many leaders. We are taught to be visionary leaders, strong leaders, decisive leaders, and motivating leaders. How do we do this and stay humble? The answer is simple: humility makes us visionary, strong, decisive, and motivating. It's only those who don't understand humility who think humility means being weak.

To be a humble leader means to be rooted in prayer and discernment. It means being a leader who has a vision for what God is calling us to do. It means being a leader who is strong enough to hold onto that vision in the midst of other peoples' doubts and derision. It means being decisive enough to say, "This is what we have to do to be true to God's call." And it means being motivating enough to gently but firmly encourage others to follow God's direction.

The key is that we can't discover God's direction if we are arrogant, because being arrogant leads us to be ignorant of God's will. Arrogance only has room for our will. This brings us back to a primary problem in modern church leadership. We have too many pastors who display one of two kinds of arrogance.

The first is more obvious. We see it in leaders who try to create churches, ministries, or missions as monuments to themselves. They can be great at building up churches, ministries, or missions, but the real focus is themselves. And we can tell because they measure everything in terms of quantities—how big, how many, how much, how popular.

The second is less obvious. We see a kind of wounded arrogance in leaders who are constantly frustrated by the seeming unwillingness of others to follow them. They quietly seethe behind the scenes because members aren't following enough, doing enough, giving enough, showing up enough, or being enough. They also measure things in quantities, but their arrogance is in thinking that they are the only ones who are right. The failure of everyone else to build up these quantities is constant evidence to them that everyone else is subverting their godly leadership: "How dare they subvert me when I'm the one who really knows what God wants!" As one pastor I know said to his board when they wouldn't do his bidding, "I know what God wants, you don't. I went to seminary. I know how to discern. You just need to follow God's will."

All of these are the reasons Plastow's book is going to be such a help to you. Becoming a humble leader means threading a needle. It means finding that right path where we are able to put God's will first, but even more to put God's results first. We don't create edifices for ourselves or rant and rave about the failure to have an edifice built. Instead we become people willing to serve God with compassion, sacrificial service, openness, brokenness, self-awareness, forgiveness, and gratitude.

As you read through these pages, you will be deepened by God to find a new way of leadership that opens up whole new realms of ministry and mission. This is done by rooting ourselves in God's calling rather than our own ambitions. It opens up a path to a partnership between us and Christ that allows Christ's Spirit to come alive in us so that the Spirit can work through us.

My hope and blessing is that as you read these pages, you will find a new path for your own leadership that is filled with grace and peace and light and love.

The Rev. N. Graham Standish, Ph.D., M.S.W.
Executive Director
Samaritan Counseling Center
Sewickley, Pennsylvania
Author of *Humble Leadership*

Foreword by Pastor Arron Chambers

One time, my friend Brent gave me great advice that I think about almost every day. He told me that I should take humility wherever I can find it.

Where do you find humility?

- the mirror?
- the gym?
- work?
- at the doctor's office?
- through your spouse?

President Theodore Roosevelt found humility in looking at the stars.

William Beebe, the naturalist, used to tell this story about former President Teddy Roosevelt. Beebe said that, while visiting President Roosevelt at his home, Sagamore Hill, often—after an evening of talk—the two would go out on the lawn and search the skies for a certain spot of star-like light near the lower left-hand corner of the Great Square of Pegasus. At this point, Roosevelt would recite: "That is the Spiral Galaxy in Andromeda. It is as large as our Milky Way. It is one of a hundred million galaxies. It consists of one hundred billion suns, each larger than our sun." Then Roosevelt would grin and say, "Now I think we are small enough! Let's go to bed." Teddy Roosevelt found humility by looking at the stars.

I find humility by looking at Jesus.

Throughout his ministry Jesus taught about the importance of humility. In Luke 14, when dealing with Pharisees who were putting their own interests before the interests of the people they were supposed to be reaching, Jesus said,

**For everyone who exalts himself will be humbled, and he who humbles himself will be exalted"
(Luke 14:11).**

I also find humility in this book and in its author, Dr. John Plastow.

In *The Humility Factor*, as he points to Jesus as the model for humility, Dr. John Plastow clearly and skillfully leads the reader through an insightful study of the issue of humility and emphasizes the importance of humility in the context of leadership. With specific data, biblical illustrations, and lots of life experience, John provides a resource that has the power to raise up a generation of more humble leaders leading more healthy churches.

If you are looking for humility, you will find it in Dr. John Plastow and in this wonderful book he's written.

Blessings,

    Arron Chambers
    Lead Minister, Journey Christian Church
    Author of *Eats With Sinners*

PREFACE

Promptings

One might wonder, what would prompt someone to write a book on humility? Especially in this culture of self-promotion, inflated egos, and celebrity status-seeking, even among pastors who have publicly expressed their commitment to spreading the good news of Jesus, humility is not usually high on the list of attention-getting goals which pastors aspire to reach, nor an ambitious state to be sought after and realized. Let's face it. Humble is just not sexy. It typically does not capture the spotlight nor draw large crowds of people to a church, where they will dwell on every word one preaches. There are examples of humble pastors who are doing the work of Christ excellently and have growing vibrant churches, but don't expect to hear about it from them. They quietly continue to faithfully execute their calling, trusting that their actions will speak for themselves and that God will bless them as He sees fit.

These churches and their pastors are highly effective and might be considered "successful" in the world's eyes because they choose to follow Christ's example of humility as found in scripture:

Though he [Jesus] was in the form of God, did not count equality with God a thing to be grasped, but emptied himself, by taking the form of a servant, being born in the likeness of men.

And being found in human form, he humbled himself by becoming obedient to the point of death, even death on a cross.[1]

These pastors authentically consider humility above hubris, calling above celebrity, and kingdom impact above personal reward. They possess the qualities found in what I call the humility factor, as modeled by Jesus, which leads them to a state of humble intelligence, equipping them to lead their churches in a manner that is not always common today. This book is about them and how church lay leaders can identify these qualities, then hire and develop such a leader.

I write this book because of various promptings. First, I have been a staff pastor for 25 years, in some capacity of ministry for nearly four decades, and, as scary as it may sound, have spent my entire life in the church! My father was a senior pastor and I personally answered the call to ministry right out of college. I have seen the very best in church people, the worst, and everything in between. I don't always understand why God chose the church to do His work on earth, but He did, and He obviously loves every one of them and every person who walks through the doors.

However, one thing I have learned is that church work is not for the faint of heart. There are certainly many mountaintop experiences, but there are also the valleys and the challenges and heartache that come from working with imperfect people and doing tasks which are often unnoticed and underappreciated. My dad used to say to me, "Church work would be easy if it weren't for the people!" I know that his tongue-in-cheek comment was primarily referring to the people in the pews, but most of us who have worked on a staff at a local church understand that sometimes the most difficult people in a church with whom to deal are the others on staff, including the lead pastor. As you read this book, I will share many of my experiences, good and bad, from my perspective of being on the inside of pastoral ministry.

The next prompting for this book came from a life-changing experience I had when I discovered the book *Humble Leadership* written by Pastor Graham Standish. Early in my Master's degree studies, I was searching for support for my premise that the way many churches were being led, through a top-down hierarchy model, could be improved in favor of a more collaborative team approach. In my research, I came across a book review of Standish's book that included statements that instantly resonated with me, and I ordered the book immediately. Upon reading the whole book, I was captivated by the approach to collaboration and Spirit-active leadership,[2] but mostly by the in-depth discussion of what a humble leader looks like in their attitudes, behaviors, and the way they interact with others in a church setting. I became a raving fan, so many of the concepts presented in this book grew from the seeds planted by Pastor Standish. I will share many of his thoughts throughout this book.

Finally, I write this book because I feel God's calling on my life to be helpful to churches. Due to my lifelong experience in the church, I have a unique perspective to see ways in which the church and its pastors can do things better. Please understand, though, that the concepts I will share are not meant as a criticism of the church that Jesus loves, because I, too, love the church and its people. They are also not meant to imply that I am any less fallible than others in pastoral ministry, but rather, to help recognize that sometimes we church leaders fall short of the example Jesus provided in how to be a humble leader. I am the last one to say that I have gotten it all correct – just ask any of the thousand or so volunteers I've worked with directly over the years. There have been many times in my ministry in which I failed miserably in following Christ's model, so I do not intend to boast that I have it all together. I am a fellow journeyman in the very difficult task of leading God's people; however, I have a profound sense of calling to share my experiences, observations, and revelations about how Jesus would have pastors lead. I sincerely want to be helpful and assist church lay leaders to hire and develop pastors who will lead with humility. We are on this journey to humble intelligence together. Let's begin with our first true life story.

CHAPTER 1

Healthy Churches are Led by Humble Pastors

Introduction

An Affair to Remember

It was a Saturday evening and the multi-purpose room of the church was filled with people who came that evening to put on a unique prom for a group of adults with special needs from throughout the community. Dressed in their best clothes, the honored guests were each assigned a "buddy" from the church's team of volunteers, who would be their "date" for the evening. The room was decorated as one would expect a prom to be: with tablecloths, place settings, streamers, and a DJ's flashing lights. The house lights were dimmed and above the dance floor were dozens of individually lit globes that gave the room a warm glow and ambiance. The guests were served dinner by a team of well-dressed servers whose only purpose was to make sure the guests felt valued and welcome. Everyone was served a meal fit for the prom's royal court of a sandwich provided by the nearby Chick-fil-A, chips, soda, cookies, and cake. It may not sound like a gourmet meal, but it's exactly what this group wanted! The food was abundant and many guests took advantage of seconds, served on silver trays. After dinner, the dancing began.

In the next room was another banquet being served to the caregivers of the adults with special needs. In this case, they were treated to specially-prepared pasta and chicken, served by another group of well-dressed food servers from the church, and given the opportunity to relax and enjoy a few minutes of rest away from the constancy of their nearly 24/7 service to the adults next door. As they enjoyed the fellowship and good food, raffle tickets were distributed and prizes were given out. As a special treat, four chair massage stations were made available by local massage therapists who volunteered their time.

The evening went on for over three hours as the people in both rooms thoroughly enjoyed the night of pampering and festivities. The main room was in motion the entire time as the guests danced with their buddies, song after song, with no break in the music. Even the Chick-fil-A mascot got into the action and danced the night away with anyone who desired a dance with a cow!

In addition to all of the church volunteers dancing with their guests was the pastor, also a buddy for the night. He wasn't there to preach a sermon or act as an emcee. He didn't parade around and make himself known. Rather, he stayed with his assigned date and danced, and danced, and danced. The only time he spoke on the microphone was to introduce one of the guests who had decided to make the prom the moment where he promised himself to his girlfriend, also a guest that evening. If you didn't know that the pastor was the pastor, there was nothing to indicate his position at the church. For that event, he was just someone showing the love of Jesus to someone who needed to be told that they were special, and as the pastor modeled, so went the rest of the people of the church that night.

I spent the evening on the kitchen team, which arrived prior to the event to set up for the food service, get drinks into ice, and make sure that the tables were set in both rooms for the special guests and the caregivers. I was impressed with the generous spirit of all of the volunteers, and especially the leaders of the event, who, if you didn't know they were the leaders, you would think were just other members of the team. Everyone worked side by side to make sure everything was ready when the doors opened to the guests. Soon the rooms were full of people and activity, which was our cue to get the food out of the kitchen and to the excited and grateful group of people upon whom the whole event was focused.

While one team served the caregivers, my team served the sandwiches, chips, drinks, cookies, and cake to the adults with special needs, all of whom were enthusiastic and visibly delighted to be in attendance. There were plenty of sandwiches, so many took advantage of seconds, and a few asked for one for later, placing it in their coat pocket, while several took enough to share their midnight snack with friends. What was striking to me is that everyone we served was extremely grateful and gracious, often going out of their way to make sure their friends were taken care of, happy, content, and full! Within only a few minutes after the meal was served, people were up and dancing, guests and buddies enjoying themselves equally. I spent the next three hours serving tables, picking up trash, and making sure that no need was left unmet. It was a great, though exhausting, experience and one which the guests and the volunteers who made it happen will never forget. In addition, while the foundational motivation was to serve the guests and their caregivers, the church also reaped untold benefits in the community long term.

⋏ ⋏ ⋏

The prom was a huge success and is an annual event for the church. However, just as with the pastor, if you didn't know it was happening, you would not have known outside the church walls, because this church has no interest in publicity. They do this event for one reason, to show the love of Jesus to people who are rarely told they are loved and special. Other than internal recruiting for the event and a subtle event description on the website and their Facebook page, this event was off the radar.

This is the culture of this particular church, which is a reflection of the lead pastor, who, though highly accomplished in his ministry of preaching and writing, chooses to remain in the background, seeking little, if any, public acknowledgment of the work of Jesus which he does. He is a humble pastor, and his church is a humble church. Both are highly effective, and many would argue successful, but the motive, rhetoric, and actions are intentionally those which were modeled by Jesus, who, though deserving of the highest honor, humbled Himself to the point of death on a cross.

Here's the point. If we want healthy churches that relentlessly show the love of Christ, they must be led by humble pastors.

It doesn't matter the size, scope, or perceived success of the church, because church health is not measured by worldly metrics, but rather through the lens of God's call to spread His message of love to all as displayed by their words and actions, and more importantly, by the motives held within the hearts of the people, especially their lead pastor. Any level of selfish ambition decreases the integrity of the pastor's work, and unyielded pride ultimately disqualifies even the most apparently qualified leader for God's blessing. Though growth, fame and even riches may befall a church led by a skilled, charismatic, and charming, but egocentric leader, the health of the church will gradually rot from the inside out, eventually leaving a hollow shell which touts good works and sprawling facilities, but is devoid of the true heart and Spirit of God.

What must church congregations look for when hiring their next lead pastor? What is missing? It is the humility factor.

So What?

At this point you may be saying to yourself, "So what, who cares?" You may agree that the church described did a good thing for their community and that God was most likely pleased with their reasons for presenting such an event, but how does this apply to my church and my pastor? The answer lies in motive. We must examine why this activity was dreamed up in the first place and how it was executed. For whose benefit was the event intended and for whose glory was it carried out? In this case, the church, which is consistently highly intentional about being the hands and feet of Jesus without overtly seeking public attention, went through months of preparation and executed the evening solely for the benefit of their guests, and then sincerely gave all glory and credit to God, even though they could have used this event to further their notoriety and reputation in the community. It could have been done strictly with the hope to attract people to visit their church. However, while their stock in the eyes of many rises each time they serve the community in this way, the church chooses to take the humble path of sacrificial service, allowing God to determine the blessing and reward which comes to them.

It should be said at this point that I don't believe there is anything wrong with a church promoting events and doing things to draw appropriate attention to itself when the motive is right. There must be consistent and intentional effort given to let the community know that they exist and that they would love for people to come and join in the good things that they have to offer. Throughout my entire ministry, part of my duties has been to help spread the word about the church I was serving and do what I could do to entice people to visit. I have even been affectionately referred to as "having the spiritual gift of hype," so for me to say that churches should not advertise or promote themselves would be hypocritical. I've done every appropriate form of promotion you can think of, from traditional media outlets to radio and television interviews, billboards, banners, movie theatre pre-show commercials, and of course, social media. I know how to generate attention; just ask anyone who has ever worked with me. However, the point here is that self-promotion for a church or a pastor should not be the first motive for doing good works. It must be way down the list of priorities when doing the work of ministry.

In a 2015 article, Ron Edmondson states, "In the day of platform-building and social media, the more we promote ourselves online, the more the characteristic of humility is being forgotten and certainly less embraced."[3] I could not agree more, and I hope to help you understand how important it is that our motives are pure and that we do our work with humility, which Standish states, "is among the hardest of all virtues because it requires that we willingly put aside ego and pride to embrace meekness."[4] Unfortunately, not many congregations would include "meek" on their wish list for a new lead pastor. Later in this book, we will discuss the results of a survey of congregation members who were asked what they believe should be the top attributes of a lead pastor, as well as what current lead pastors believe are the most highly desirable traits. Spoiler alert: Meek was not a word used by anyone.

Successful, Effective, Healthy

It is reasonable to assume that in most cases, churches want to be 1) successful, 2) effective, and 3) healthy. I define these terms below.

A church is typically considered successful when it has strong and growing attendance at services, can pay their bills with enough left over for a reserve account and monies available for special projects and missions as needs arise, and has a regular flow of visitors who like what they experience and stick around. In addition, successful churches have a great reputation in the community, enjoy positive exposure, have a competent and caring professional staff, and are known for programs and ministries that are unique to them.

Effective has two definitions when it comes to churches. First and foremost, an effective church is one that fulfills the great commandment and the great commission outlined in scripture. Jesus commanded us to "Love the Lord your God with all your heart and with all your soul and with all your mind. And you shall love your neighbor as yourself."[5] Then He commissioned us to "Go and make disciples of all nations, baptizing them in the name of the Father, the Son, and the Holy Spirit, teaching them to observe all that I have commanded you."[6] When a church truly loves God, loves people, and intentionally draws people to a relationship with Jesus Christ, they are biblically effective. The second definition is more from a community perspective, in that if a church has quality programming and events that draw large crowds and is visibly meeting the real and perceived needs of individual people and groups, they are considered effective.

Healthy is the most challenging of the three to define and identify, because it is possible for a church to meet the above criteria for being successful and effective, but, out of the general view of the public, suffer from broken relationships, power struggles, and incongruence of espoused values and priorities with behavior, moral failures, and self-ambition. These stem from what C. S. Lewis describes when he states, "Pride leads to every other vice: It is the complete anti-God state of mind."[7] In other words, when there is a lack of humility, or pride, on the part of the leaders of a church, it opens the door for all kinds of unhealthy behavior.

Healthy churches put the needs of people first, treat everyone with love and grace, and direct all honor to God and God alone. For a church to be healthy, it must be humble, and because all organizations are a reflection of their leader, if the leader is filled with pride and ambition, as warned against by the apostle Paul when he states, "Do nothing from selfish ambition or conceit, but in humility count others more significant than yourselves,"[8] or suffers from other vices, the church, too, will be lacking in humility and in health. It all comes from the leader. No humility, no health. As my friend Ray Johnston of Bayside Church in Granite Bay, CA, often states, "It all comes down to leadership." Churches that desire to be healthy must have a healthy and humble pastor because, as Standish states, "When we lead from a sense of humility, willingly putting aside our own motivations and desires in favor of God's call, we create the context in which people are more willing to put aside their own will to seek God's will."[9] Simply stated, healthy churches are led by humble pastors.

Churches Need Strong Leaders, but...
According to Bonem and Patterson, "Effectively leading the average congregation in America is every bit as challenging as corporate leadership,"[10] so it stands to reason that churches need

strong pastors who are skilled, gifted, accomplished, and driven in order for them to help their church to be successful by the above definition. They also must be strategic, focused, passionate, and committed in order to be effective. However, humility is rapidly being identified by scholars and practitioners as a must-have trait in leaders[11] because it provides the foundations of moral strength, valor, excellence, and worth[12] and is generally viewed as something that is good and human, and produces a better society.[13] It also compels people to follow you! As Hartwig and Bird state, "There cannot be genuine servant leadership apart from genuine humility. To the degree that your team sees and believes that, they will want to follow you."[14]

Humility Toward God

We will discuss at length the qualities which are evident in a pastor with humble intelligence in chapter three. For now, this kind of leader begins with an understanding of who one is in comparison to God Almighty. Pastor Douglas Hall states, "We are living in an illusion if we think that our organizations [churches] or programs alone are causing anything that relates to God's ultimate purposes to happen at the significant level that God expects."[15] Let's face it, regardless of our accomplishments, if we were to ask our closest friends what they think of us, they are probably not in awe of us![16] So what most of us really need to do is get over ourselves, because none of us are "all that," especially when we compare ourselves to God. He trumps us every time! Church leadership coach Greg Atkinson says this well when he writes,

> Some of the best advice someone gave me years ago was to not take myself too seriously. [I needed] a Christ-centered, God-sized view of who I am and Who He is. This concept is especially challenging for gifted and talented

individuals. Some pastors can really preach. Some worship leaders are very good musicians. Some video editors have mad skills. The point is a lot of church leaders are talented and it's easy to see why they wrestle with staying humble.

The problem is when we start relying on our strength, skills and ability and stop praying for Christ through the Holy Spirit to lead through us, preach and teach through us, sing and play through us, edit and design through us. We must have the perspective of vessels, jars of clay and a heavenly potter sculpting us and shaping us for great things according to His plans and His purpose.[17]

I really appreciate this perspective because I have spent most of my ministry surrounded by highly gifted and very talented people. I've had the privilege of working with some of the greatest singers, dancers, actors, and technical artists the Lord has equipped for His work in churches all over the country, and what separates many of them from others is their attitude toward their gifting. Some believe they stand out above the rest because of their own efforts, but others remain humble servants. Pastor Graham Standish identifies this well when he states,

> We are distinct and special not because of any qualities or abilities we ourselves possess. Our unique qualities are gifts from God that come from God's Spirit breathed into us…nothing we do by our own power. The humble person sees their ability as a gift from God, not as evidence of personal greatness.[18]

Wow! That will sure put us in our place when we start to think that we're responsible for the talents and gifts we have when, in fact, Christ Himself is the giver of all gifts, which are given specifically to help build the church and for us to grow in Christ-likeness. When speaking of our gifts, there is no place for human pride.[19] We must always remember that we didn't create ourselves and that the old-school "self-made man (or woman)" is at best a myth, or at worst, a recipe for an ego out of control. We must remember that God is great and we are not, but God can do great things through us if we let Him do so.

The apostle Paul writes, "For the wisdom of this world is folly with God,"[20] meaning that it really doesn't matter how talented, educated, or intelligent someone is, they do not hold a candle to God! It is important that pastors understand this. They must lead with humility, understanding that this means leading from the ground and from the bottom up,[21] allowing God to be in control of their church. They are to do as the great kings of Israel did, "Have a humble dependence on God"[22] and be radically open to His guidance.[23] The church needs leaders who will subjugate their agenda to God with the understanding that glory, honor, praise, and credit belong to Him and Him only. How do we do that? Let's look at the ultimate role model set by Jesus.[24]

Jesus: Humble Servant

Jesus is often referred to as the greatest example of servant leadership to have ever lived.[25] In His own countercultural manner,[26] He went about His ministry serving the people He encountered in whatever way was needed at the moment. Healing, encouragement, forgiveness, provision, and care were all ways in which Jesus served people even while possessing the power to do whatever He might choose to do at any given time.[27] However, instead of overturning governments and flexing His creator-of-the-universe muscles, He washed feet, wept with beloved friends, and provided wine at a wedding party.

DR. JOHN PLASTOW

Author of *Love Does*, a fantastic book about authentic Christian compassion, Bob Goff, states,

> In a world driven by self-promotion and spin, Jesus modeled something different for us. Jesus was saying that instead of telling people about what we're doing all the time, there's a better way. One that doesn't require any capes that can get snagged on something—something like ourselves. Maybe Jesus wants us to be secretly incredible instead. That was His plan for self-promotion. Secretly incredible people keep what they do one of God's best-kept secrets because the only one who needs to know, the God of the universe, already knows.[28]

Jesus was that way. It was not unusual for Jesus to do something miraculous, and then say, "Tell no one," as in the story told in Luke 8 when a ruler had been told that his daughter had died.

> But Jesus, on hearing this, answered him, "Do not fear; only believe, and she will be well." And when he came to the house, he allowed no one to enter with him, except Peter and John and James, and the father and mother of the child. And all were weeping and mourning for her, but he said, "Do not weep, for she is not dead but sleeping." And they laughed at him, knowing that she was dead. But taking her by the hand he called, saying, "Child, arise." And her spirit returned, and she got up at once. And he directed that something should be given to her to eat. And her parents were amazed, but he charged them to tell no one what had happened.[29]

Imagine for a moment how difficult it would be for the parents to keep the miracle of their daughter being brought back to life to themselves, but even more so, imagine how difficult it would be for any of us to keep secret something so miraculous that we had done ... but that's what Jesus did. Our nature is one which craves attention, and when we do something great, we want not only the respect and rewards, but also the credit. The model we see in Jesus is that He always gave credit to the source, God the Father, and He rarely broadcast his accomplishments. Bob Goff speaks of this as well.

> Jesus hardly talked to anyone about what He'd done. The Bible never depicts one of those end-of-camp slideshows where Jesus goes over all He had done with His disciples. Instead, Jesus modeled that we don't need to talk about everything we've done.[30]

Think back to the opening story of this book, which showed how a church pastor chose to keep his accomplishments and activities quiet. This is a prime example of how our modern-day churches can follow the example set by Christ.

It is understood that almost all of us would prefer to think of ourselves more as movers and shakers than as servants. We are attracted to reputation, position, and power far more than redemptive servitude,[31] but when we look at Jesus' example, we must recognize that if He, being God, didn't seek the recognition, fame, and fortune while He was on this earth, how can we? Jesus was a humble servant of the Heavenly Father, and so, too, must we be.

What's the Point? What's at Stake? What's Missing?

There is no argument with the fact that the local church needs to have competent, passionate, and committed individuals leading their congregations. Today's churches must have someone at the helm who can navigate the challenges of contemporary culture relevance, ambiguity, and the pressures of finances, balance, and competition for people's attention and time. Pastors who want their churches to thrive must be a blend of entrepreneur, CEO, scholar, and shepherd. They must lead, so their leadership competence matters big time, but it is not all that matters.[32] It's important to keep in mind that for Jesus, "the mark of true leadership is humility."[33] He said,

> You know that the rulers of the Gentiles lord it over them, and their great ones exercise authority over them. It shall not be so among you. But whoever would be great among you must be your servant and whoever would be first among you must be your slave.[34]

Unfortunately, being a slave is not what many pastors have in mind as they bound out of Bible school and accept their first assignment. Leadership, influence, recognition, achievement, yes. But slavery? Not so much. I've heard lead pastors say that they wanted to be the lead so that they could "call the shots, do things their way, be in charge," and even to "make more money." None of these reasons are the words of a slave of Christ. However, a really important thing to understand is that it's not entirely their fault, because many churches set their pastors up to become anything but humble, pouring out the accolades in words and rewards to the point that pastors start to believe that they are as great as their followers say they are. It's no wonder that their egos get out of line when people treat them as though they are the anointed messengers of God and the alpha and the omega of church leadership. When people dwell on every word that is spoken and fawn over every deed that is done, it's easy for the recipient to start down the path of self-importance and pride, forgetting that they began this journey by answering the call to serve God by spreading the good news and taking care of people. In the book *Spiritual Leadership*, Sanders provides a strong and chilling warning about pride that we must consider.

> Pride: When a person rises in position, as happens to leaders in the church, the tendency to pride also increases. If not checked, the attitude will disqualify the person from further advancement in the kingdom of God, for "the LORD detests all the proud of heart."[35] These are strong and searching words! Nothing aggravates God more than conceit, the sin that aims at setting the self upon a throne, making of God a secondary figure. That very sin changed the anointed cherub into the foul fiend of hell."[36]

These are strong words every pastor should heed; however, the real problem doesn't begin with the pastor, but rather the people who hire them. A problem exists in many churches, particularly when a church has gone through some difficulties and decline. Church lay leaders who are desperate to turn the church around will often look to hire an individual who can make them successful and effective, but miss the greater need to be healthy and humble as described above. They look to hire a CEO type who will help them improve their market share, bring in more capital, restructure the staff to be more efficient, and be a transformational leader who will turn them into the next powerhouse and make their church a trending topic on social media, much like their secular-world counterparts. Dan Kimball identifies this trend as beginning in the 1980s, when "churches began applying business principles to the church. Pastors and leaders began using some of the language and metaphors of the business world, including business descriptions to titles."[37] These objectives are not entirely wrong, but they cannot be the only things considered when hiring a new pastor. Even though good business principles should be a part of the administration of the church, there are some inherent problems that arise when lay leaders decide to "run the church like a business."

▲ ▲ ▲

Family Church's Painful Transition

Family Church was healthy and prosperous. It had a nearly 100-year history and had tripled in size over two decades and moved into a prominent and spacious new facility with high visibility in the community. There was no reason to believe that the church would do anything but continue to enjoy the blessings of God as it looked forward to the succession of a new lead pastor. With this event only a few years away, the current pastor, being highly influenced by successful business people within the congregation, hired an outside consultant to perform an analysis of the current strengths and weaknesses of the organization, clarify its mission and values, and set objectives for the future. The "real world" business consultant was also charged with assisting the senior leader with the complex process of achieving a successful succession to an already-identified new leader.

For nearly two years the process of analysis, mission clarification, rebranding, and the implementation of comprehensive organizational restructuring took place, with the consultant being given broad influence in the decisions being made because of their extensive and successful experience in the secular business world. Generally, advice given and actions taken were sound and appropriate in an organizational context; however, as time progressed, it became evident that while the consultant was well-qualified and effective for a business environment, they lacked certain insights due to an incongruence of faith, a misunderstanding of the church's biblical values, and a lack of concern for the heritage of the church – a concern which is particularly important to churches. In the end, broad change initiatives were implemented and the succession completed, and the church has remained strong; however, not without the casualties of broken relationships, the loss of talented staff, and the departure of long-time members. Today Family Church is considered successful and effective, but only after a painful transition.[38] If they could go back and do things differently, they might consider a more compassionate approach to organizational change, a much higher degree of communication with all stakeholders, and a greater commitment to insuring relationships remained healthy within the family.

▲ ▲ ▲

Caution: The Dark Side

The case study above described the negative situation which arose during the selection and hiring of a consultant at Family Church. Caution must be observed by churches regarding a dark side which can arise when church leaders choose to hire someone who is not aligned with the church's values, views, and mission, or when there is a lack of knowledge and understanding of how a church functions, not only from a standpoint of the heritage of the local ministry, but also according to biblical guidelines. "Values are generally defined as an enduring belief that a specific mode of conduct or end-state of existence is personally or socially preferable."[39] This concept also applies in an organizational context, especially to churches, and in this case, values were not fully shared.

A "permanent dilemma of congruence"[40] occurs when the church and the consultant do not share similar beliefs and values and can result in decisions being implemented in ways that run contrary to the servant leadership modeled by Jesus. While the concepts of rightsizing an organization [41] and assembling the right team, or getting the right people on the bus,[42] are applicable to both secular- and faith-based organizations, the ways they are implemented are quite different. Compassion and care take on greater importance in an organization such as a church that espouses its priority as the welfare of its people, as does the understanding that churches are sacred places in which people, purposes, and property must be treated differently than at most businesses in the marketplace.[43]

There is no doubt that churches can and should benefit from pastors who have keen business minds and experience. Unfortunately, though, the price tag attached to hiring such a strong leader is often the giving of unconditional power and a lessening of accountability, which sows the seeds for leaders to become intoxicated with their position of unquestioned influence and forget that they were called to be servants. Author Gerald Keucher states,

> The important thing to remember about servants is that, of all people, they are always completely accountable to those they serve. Servants are told what to do, so if no one can tell you what to do, you are not a servant, but a master.[44]

Sadly, I have known pastors who believe that no one can or should be able to tell them what to do, and too many lay leaders have abdicated their responsibility to hold their pastor accountable, allowing them to hire and fire at will, initiate massive organizational change without regard to the general constituency, and disrespect the heritage of the church by marginalizing staff members who don't fit the "new profile," pushing aside people who have been faithful to the ministry over the long haul. In addition, when someone has unchallenged power, it will often lead to a host of other unhealthy, self-indulgent behaviors that can literally destroy a church and leave a once-effective ministry in shambles, as is the case in the next examples.

When Egos Run Amuck

This is well documented in the demise of once-impactful ministries led by gifted communicators, charismatic leaders, and focused strategists who founded churches which would become players on the world stage. While there are many examples, there are two in particular that fell, at least in part, because of out-of-control, egotistical leaders who had been given complete authority to do as they saw fit in the building of ministry empires, with little or no accountability. Because of their personal fame and the notoriety and success it brought to the church, their behaviors of self-aggrandizement, self-indulgence, dictatorship, organizational bullying, and moral indiscretions appear to have been ignored by the people who were supposed to be overseeing the ministry. Poor behavior was tolerated because the church was successful; however, eventually their lack of humility, which led to other vices, caught up with each.

Beginning in the 1960s and continuing into the 1980s, Jim and Tammy Faye Bakker ruled as king and queen of Christian televangelists – until their empire came crashing down, according to columnist Sherryl Connelly of the *New York Daily News*. She reports ugly sexual revelations, including hush money doled out to a sultry church secretary, and financial revelations exposing the exorbitant sums the couple spent on furs, diamonds, and luxury cars. In 1989, Jim went to prison for defrauding the faithful of $158 million,[45] and also disgraced by sexual scandal. He served his time and today he is remarried and back on the air.

Another example, though quite different than the above, was the resignation of Mark Driscoll, the successful long-term pastor of Mars Hill Church in Seattle, WA, as reported by *Christianity Today* in 2014. In a statement following the receipt of the resignation, the board stated,

"Driscoll had been guilty of arrogance, responding to conflict with a quick temper and harsh speech, and leading the staff and elders in a domineering manner." Most of the charges involved attitudes and behaviors reflected by a domineering style of leadership.[46]

▲ ▲ ▲

A year after Driscoll's resignation, I had the opportunity to hear him speak at a church leadership conference, where he had the chance to clear the air of what had happened from his perspective. The audience was made up mostly of pastors who, while cautious about giving too much immediate grace, seemed to collectively want to give him a chance to redeem himself and hoped that he would. They listened intently as he spoke. While he did appear to be less audaciously driven and commanding, it was disappointing to those whom I was with and me that he had not entirely allowed the experience to change him, at least to the point of taking responsibility for being the bullying type of leader that the people who had worked with him said he had been. Unfortunately, redemption, at least in the eyes of his peers, did not happen that night. At best, it was the smallest of baby steps on the long road to restoration. Only time will tell if he is truly restored.

Ultimately, both of these men paid a great price for their arrogance, pride, and other failures, and both have since begun other ministries. Bakker is operating out of Branson, MO, and is said to be doing quite well for himself, while Driscoll has planted a new church in Scottsdale, AZ, and appears to have returned to a more biblically-authentic way of doing church ministry, at least on the surface. Truly, only God can judge each of these pastors, but they are good examples of what can happen when pride and ego take control. These are extreme examples with megachurch pastors; however, churches of any size can suffer the devastation that comes from an unaccountable leader who is allowed to do as they please in the name of church success. Lay leaders must watch their pastor so that this doesn't happen to their church, or better, make sure that they hire a humble pastor in the first place.

What's at Stake?

Radical, legendary, and entertaining pastor Tony Campolo wrote the book *Following Jesus Without Embarrassing God* in 1997 because he was convinced that one of the biggest things working against winning people to Jesus was Christians themselves. He states,

> It's one thing for the world to reject Jesus because the people in secular society consider the gospel to be ridiculous. It is quite another thing for the world to reject the gospel because Christians are an embarrassment to God.[47]

In the two decades since Campolo wrote those words, the topic of how Christians hurt the Christian cause has been written about numerous times, including in Bickel and Jantz's book *I'm Fine With*

God...It's Christians I Can't Stand. In it, they state, "Every segment of society has its members of the lunatic fringe but Christianity seems to have a disproportionately high percentage of them."[48] Kimball's book discussing how to reach emerging generations, *They Like Jesus But Not the Church*, states, "Today, Christians are known as scary, angry, judgmental, right-wing finger-pointers with political agendas."[49]

What comes to mind in these descriptions may be the street-corner loudmouth bent on shouting judgment and condemnation to passersby, all in the name of speaking the truth, or perhaps the one who holds the John 3:16 sign in the stands at sporting events, convinced that merely seeing the scripture will compel someone to come to a relationship with Jesus. I guess it's possible that people have responded to these Christian zealots; however, I've never met one or heard a story of one. These extremists have been pointed to as part of what turns people off to Christianity, but the damage they do in the kingdom pales in comparison to egocentric, opulent, self-righteous, and uncaring pastors. These pastors are the real reason why so many are not only leaving the church of their parents, but becoming anti-Christian altogether. Kimball quotes someone who left Christianity behind as saying,

> I would be totally into going to a church if the church revolved more around the person of Jesus than around the personality of the pastor. I'd be totally interested in going if the church were more about helping and loving other people than about criticizing and condemning other people.[50]

What's at stake is peoples' eternal lives, and many are no longer open to the gospel simply because they are disgusted and disillusioned by pastors whom they consider hypocritical.

Here are some statistics which make all of this discussion particularly alarming.

- According to the Shaping Tomorrow website, the weekend attendance percentage at evangelical churches fell below 9% of the United States population for the first time in 2010 and is expected to fall to 8.5% by 2020.[51]
- This same trend is even more alarming in Europe, as only 1.4% of the English population was reported to attend weekly services in 2014. A 2016 headline of one European Christian publication reads, "Christianity is Dying in Europe: Lowest Church Attendance Ever."[52]
- The website of Religious Tolerance projects that by 2030, Christianity will become a minority religion in the United States.[53]
- According to the Pew Research Center, one of the projected major shifts in people's participation in religion in the United States will be from "Christianity" to "Unaffiliated," which will go from 16% in 2010 to 26% in 2050.
- By 2070 Christianity and Islam will be in parity, with Islam becoming the largest religion in the world by 2100.[54]

These statistics show that there are definite casualties when there is a disconnect between what pastors and churches say they believe and stand for, such as the love of all people, and their actions, such as public condemnation of people with whom they disagree. Another example would be a pastor who insists people give so that the church can take care of the poor, all the while driving one of several new and expensive cars around town.

Another casualty manifests itself in the church's diminished community relations. There was a time when the general culture and community members gave churches the benefit of the doubt when they observed what might be considered an inconsistency between message and behavior. However, as society has become less and less sympathetic to the mission of the church and more skeptical about the true motivations of churches, pastors, and Christians in general, the rules have changed, making it extremely important for anyone associated with a church to be practicing what it preaches, especially the senior pastor.[55] People abhor the hypocrisy that they observe when organizational behaviors are incompatible with espoused values.[56] The damage done to a church's ability to have influence in their community is monumental when the community doesn't trust, respect or even particularly care for the senior pastor.

The worst casualty of all is the cause of Christ – the many people who will never meet Jesus. The world is not going to tolerate church leaders who say one thing and do another. Even though individual non-believers may not hold themselves to the same standards, they will aggressively oppose insincere and inauthentic church leaders. In the book *The Leadership Challenge*, Kouzes & Posner state, "If people don't see a consistency, they conclude that the leader is, at best, not really serious or, at worst, an outright hypocrite."[57] When this happens, hearts close to the message of Jesus because they don't trust the messenger. The kingdom of God loses big time.[58]

What's Missing?

To reiterate the premise of this book, healthy churches are led by humble pastors. They model what it means to be humble and the church becomes a reflection of their leader, putting aside their will in favor of God's call[59] for the greater good of the people they serve and the community they are trying to reach. What's missing in many churches is not leadership skills, passion, strategy, organizational practices, innovation or communicative expertise, but rather the evidence of the humility factor on the part of the lead pastor. Standish states, "Humble leaders motivate people to follow God's vision. In contrast, conventional leaders motivate people to follow the leader's vision."[60] Achieving humble intelligence is not easy for leaders of any kind, especially pastors, because, as Keucher observes,

> The church is structured in a way that makes self-importance and feelings of entitlement an easy trap to fall into. Clergy in charge of congregations are often in the spotlight, so it is easy to begin to think that the show is about you and that you deserve the best dressing room. Even if you start off with modesty and work hard, people will begin to look to you, admire you, compliment you, and defer to you, so eventually it is easy to think you deserve that kind of reverence no matter how you act.[61]

What is the Humility Factor?

By this point, you may be asking, "All right, already, what is the humility factor? Tell me what it is and how it works!" Therefore let me introduce you to the basic principles regarding which we will go into greater detail later. Remember, the purpose of this book is to assist churches to be successful, effective, AND healthy, however, in the reverse order. Remember that for a church to be healthy, it must be humble, and a reflection of their leader, who takes to heart Philippians 2:3, where the apostle Paul states, "Do nothing from selfish ambition or conceit, but in humility count others more significant than yourselves."[62] Healthy churches put the needs of people first, treat everyone with love and grace, and direct all honor to God and God alone. Healthy churches are led by humble pastors, based on the level of the pastor's humble intelligence, which is a result of the humility factor.

Before I define those terms, let me assure you that the humility factor isn't just a manufactured grouping of nice qualities which I wish the pastors I've served possessed. Nor is humble intelligence a clever formula which I made up during halftime while watching a football game. Each is the result of nearly a decade of realization that humility is at the base of the Christian leadership modeled by Jesus, extensive research, as evidenced by the large amount of endnotes you will find at the end of this book, the exegesis of scriptures that deal with each of the seven attributes of the humility factor, field study in which I have personally observed pastors with many styles of leadership, interviews with pastors and church leaders, and an online survey of pastors and lay people who answered the question, "What qualities are most important in a lead pastor?" I will share the results of these in detail later in chapter four. Finally, a large contributor to the development of the seven attributes of the humility factor was my communication with Pastor Graham Standish himself, and the handful of pastors whom he identified as humble and with whom I had the privilege of connecting.

So as you can see, the conclusions I've drawn about the importance of pastors being humble and how they can be through the collective application of the humility factor in the form of humble intelligence is not one which I merely stumbled across. It was the result of many sources coming together and a lot of time seeking what God wanted to say through this book. When adopted alongside the basic leadership style of a pastor, these principles can make a huge difference in the health of a church, which, in turn, directly impacts the cause of Christ, and for some, where they will spend eternity.

Definition: The Humility Factor (The actions)

The humility factor consists of seven attributes of humility modeled by Jesus Christ in His actions and words. Note that these are not a list to be chosen from at the leader's discretion, but rather, all are necessary for the humility factor to be evident. The seven attributes are:

- Compassion
- Sacrificial Service
- Openness
- Brokenness
- Self-Awareness
- Forgiveness
- Gratitude

Definition: Humble Intelligence (The result)

When collectively applied to a leader's life, the seven attributes of the humility factor create what I identify as humble intelligence. Humble intelligence is the result of the humility factor actions when all are present. Furthermore, when humble intelligence is applied to any leadership style, it improves it because the leader leads more like Jesus led, which we will cover in chapter four. Through this application the end result is a humble pastor.

Next is the model upon which we will base our discussion throughout the rest of this book.

The Humility Factor Model

Premise: It is awesome how God creates all leaders uniquely for specific circumstances, and not all pastors must be or should be the same. However, all pastoral leaders should aspire to follow Jesus' example of humility in their leadership practices, which results in a healthy combination of their personal style/traits and their humble intelligence.

Hypotheses:

- When the humility factor is included in the leadership equation, everything improves. Pastors become more effective because of their heightened focus on meeting the needs of people over seeking their own benefit; their leadership inspires others to join the team and pursue God-sized initiatives; and the church becomes a place to which the community looks when something important needs to get done, and is considered with high respect and regard.
- By adding the humility factor to any leadership style, it is improved. The positive is amplified as humble intelligence enhances good qualities to become better, and the negative is lessened as humble intelligence dilutes qualities contrary to humility with the attributes of the humility factor modeled by Jesus.
- When a leader adopts the humility factor and attains humble intelligence, the result will be that they will lead more like Jesus led.

Definitions:

- The Humility Factor (HF) – Seven attributes modeled by Jesus
- Humble Intelligence (HI) – The sum of the humility factor attributes
- Leadership Style (L) – Basic qualities of the person
- Humble Pastor (HP) – The outcome of adding humble intelligence to a leadership style

Example: Add humble intelligence to an autocratic, command-and-control pastor, and they stay strong, but become compassionate and collaborative.

$$\text{Sum of HF = HI} + \text{L} = \text{HP}$$

The Humility Factor Model – Plastow (2017)

Pastors who achieve humble intelligence will continually strengthen their leadership style as they grow in the humility factor, causing them to lead more and more like Jesus led. Churches led by such a pastor will be spiritually healthy, focused on Jesus' priorities, and actively equipping future generations of humble pastors to carry on the work of Christ, unlike the pastor in the following true story.

I Want to Be the Show!

>The staff at an active and energetic church was preparing for Easter services, which went far beyond just the typical Resurrection Sunday celebrations. Palm Sunday services opened the week and were thematic, corresponding with what happened in Jesus' last days on earth. Hundreds of volunteers had been preparing for months in order to provide an outstanding and meaningful experience for everyone who would come to the church, be they regular attenders or seasonal visitors. During a staff meeting a week out from the festivities, a final walkthrough of the components of the Easter services was conducted. Keep in mind that this was the last of many planning meetings

that had taken place, each with everyone on the team contributing to the creative process. Months prior, decisions had been made as to the creative elements, worship and music, teaching points, and guest experience that would be a part of every service, and these had been revisited and fine-tuned along the way. Supposedly everyone was on board and looking forward to a great celebration. Also keep in mind that the worship arts team had done a tremendous amount of preparation for their part of the services. Over a hundred volunteers were prepped, ready and excited for Holy Week to begin.

After what was intended to be the final walkthrough, the lead pastor made a statement which basically sent the process into chaos, with only a few days left to make adjustments to the plan. He stated, speaking specifically of the Easter service, "It looks like everyone else is the show. I want to be the show." The team had to scramble and retool the services that they had thought were ready to go, and then the lead pastor announced on Facebook the night before the services began that he had decided to speak on certain themes which had nothing to do with the plans everyone had agreed to and prepared for. Needless to say, there was tension when the staff gathered the next morning in the lead pastor's private dressing room and in the services that followed. The staff members affected were noticeably out of sync and had to perform with a forced sense of enthusiasm and team spirit. Worse, though, was that when volunteers were informed of the last-minute changes to their explicitly-rehearsed presentation, they were confused as to why, and went into the service far less confident than they would have been had they been allowed to do what they had been prepared to do. In the end, much of the joy which comes from this kind of artistic and spiritual celebration was stolen by the pastor who wanted to be the show.

▲ ▲ ▲

The Purpose of This Book

Futurist James Canton writes, "The future belongs to those who can envision it,"[63] which is what I certainly hope this book will help others to do – envision a better, more humble way of leading God's people in the local church. However, Thomas Chermack, another futurist, writes, "The future often acts like a drunken monkey stung by a bee – it is confused and disturbing, and its behavior is completely unpredictable,"[64] which absolutely describes how many churches function, particularly when they are embarking on finding and hiring a new lead pastor! The reason I wrote this book is because I have spent my life in churches, in which I have observed many times that pastors, with the support of their boards, have taken roads to being successful and effective, but have, for all practical purposes, ignored the attributes of the humility factor, which would help them to be healthy as well. They miss the target because they seek personal attention, admiration, acknowledgement, and the rewards which church boards are eager to lavish on a successful pastor. Their churches miss being healthy because they are not led by a humble pastor. All too often pastors are hired and then left to their own way of doing things, which too many times leaves out the attributes of humility, which this book will discuss in detail later.

I've observed search committees and church boards celebrate as they make the hire, but then check out as if their job is done, without the need to make sure that their new pastor is more than a CEO and star performer. In the book *Teams that Thrive*, Hartwig and Bird state, "In some churches, the senior leader's authority is spiritualized, making it seem uncontestable. When a church's culture emphasizes that no authority will be shared, a leadership team will never really lead the church."[65] Kimball warns that this is a dangerous way to lead a church because when the CEO, top-down mentality creeps in, it gives too much power and control to the pastor. He states, "Power and control can corrupt even good people."[66] Board members don't intend to create a dictator-like pastoral leader, and it must be assumed that pastors themselves don't typically start out intending to seize absolute power, but unfortunately, if left unchecked, in the words of 19th century British politician Lord John Dalberg-Acton, "Absolute power corrupts absolutely."[67]

Standish discusses how, in his observation, there are too many churches led by arrogant leaders who assume that they are the only ones who know what is best for their church. He describes these pastors as believing the people they serve are "spiritual infants who are ignorant of God's desires" and that they "make the tragic assumption that he [the pastor] was the only one in the church who understands what God wanted."[68] Unfortunately, I concur with Pastor Standish, as I have personally observed this arrogant behavior in a number of pastors. I wrote this book in order to help churches identify and develop the attributes of the humility factor in their pastors, which then leads to humble intelligence on their part and ultimately in their churches.

This Book Is Written for Pastors and Lay Leaders

While I sincerely hope to appeal to pastors who might come across this book to take some time of personal reflection to see where they stand regarding the attributes of the humility factor and to adopt Jesus' model of humble service, this book is especially designed for lay leaders in the church who have the responsibility of hiring their pastors and are given the authority to hold their pastors accountable. This book will present the qualities to look for in prospective pastors that go beyond the obvious skills, gifts, and experiences any qualified candidates should have. I will provide a clear method to identify the evidence of the humility factor and tell you how to apply it to leadership qualities in order to create a better version of the leader whom you will call your pastor.

You may feel that you don't have enough time to think about any more than you already are when it comes to hiring and developing a pastor. You may want to find someone who you believe is qualified and then get out of their way and let them do their job. I understand that between the demands of work and family, there is only so much time that you can devote to this effort. However, as one of the lay leaders of the church, you are committed to doing all you can to find the right new pastor. It's possible that you are losing sleep over the task of finding the replacement for the pastor whom you've followed and loved for many years, or you have hired someone and you know that there are some things about the new pastor which need to be developed. You lie awake praying that you'll make the right decisions and that the church will be in good hands for many years to come. This book will help you. When applied to any leadership style, the principles of the humility factor will make any pastor a better leader of your church.

This book may challenge your understanding of what you should look for in your pastor. You may have been quite comfortable with a command-and-control leader about whom you didn't have to worry if they were getting things done, or you may have been aware that the previous pastor had a bit of an ego, but they were successful in filling the seats because they were a gifted communicator, so you could live with it, even though you lost some good staff members who became casualties of zealous and narcissistic behaviors.

It has been said, "Comfort is the enemy of growth,"[69] so expect this book to disrupt your comfort zone as we take on the truth of how the attributes of the humility factor are rooted in scripture and in Jesus' example of humble leadership. I will do whatever is necessary to convince you of the importance of humble intelligence in your pastor. I want to help you recognize the truth of the humility factor, "not only with the reason, but also by the heart."[70] I want us all to understand that if we have a little more humility and a little less certainty, we have the chance to be of better service to the Lord.[71] So, church lay leader, this book is written for pastors and congregation members, but especially for you.

Healthy churches are led by humble pastors.

CHAPTER 2

The Journey to Humility

My Personal Humility Journey and Lessons Learned (so far)

In the next several chapters we are going to take a deep dive into the definition of the humility factor, descriptions of 22 leadership styles found in pastors, and the mechanics of how to use the humility factor in the process of hiring your next lead pastor. It will all be very intense (and fun)! However, before we do that, I want to give you some further context of why I am writing this book through the telling of my own personal journey to humility. You may be tempted to skip over this touchy-feely section in favor of getting right to the meat of the matter, but I urge you to stay with me, because by knowing where I have come from, you will have a greater understanding of why pastors should be humble.

If I had not gone through all that I'm going to tell you, and more which I'm keeping private, I would not be who I am today. I would not have the understanding of grace which I have, nor the level of compassion I have developed over the years. Simply put, I would not be anywhere close to being humble had God not taken me on this journey, through which He has completely changed how I act, think, and minister to others. I only wish that I had had this book when I began my ministry. I wish I had already had my

"Aha" moment when I realized that life didn't revolve around me. Oh, the pain I could have avoided and the good I could have done! Had I had the understanding of the principles I will cover in this book, I would have been so much more effective along the way, people would have been served better, and relationships would have been less strained. I would have been better able to draw people to Jesus instead of repel them because my ego overshadowed my desire to share the gospel.

I wish I had had this book back then, but more than that, I wish I had understood what this book teaches. Through the process which I will describe, and even more so the actual experience I have had while writing this book, I have discovered that what I was missing as a pastor, husband, dad, and friend was humility. I wasn't a bad guy; I was just very full of myself. Who I've become is the result of years of God working in me that has allowed me to become a better version of myself, but the last few months especially have made a significant impact on me as I've done the research, prayed for the Holy Spirit's guidance, and written and rewritten the chapters in this book, trying to find the exact words God wants me to write and share with you. Through it all, I've learned that had I possessed humility early on, my life would have been richer, particularly when it comes to personal relationships which were strained because of my overconfidence and self-focus. In addition, I lost opportunities in my ministry, career, and professional interactions because I functioned as if I always had the best way of doing things. Had I known then what I know now, how different my life might have been. I wish this book had been around when I was 20!

The unfortunate thing, though, is that, knowing myself as I do, a book like this would not have caught my attention. When I was a young man I knew everything, so even though this book would have done me a great deal of good, I would not have been open to its teaching. Sadly, the only way for me to learn what I have learned is to have gone through painful experiences, many of which I caused due to my pride. I sincerely wish there had been another way for me to learn. I know that some who are more open to God's guidance than I was will learn the lessons of humility in a much less arduous process. However, I had to take the more treacherous path. I can't say that I'm glad I did, but I accept that it was the only way for God to get through my thick skull and hard heart. I had to learn humility the hard way, and in retrospect, I was missing, in part or in whole, compassion, sacrificial service, openness, brokenness, self-awareness, forgiveness, and gratitude. In humility, I tell you the story of my journey to humility, which is still unfolding.

In the book *Work: A Kingdom Perspective on Labor*, Ben Witherington III states, "The sooner we swallow our humility pills and see ourselves as lowly junior partners and co-laborers with God, rather than the only laborers on the scene, the sooner we will have a real grasp of work, vocation, and calling."[72] This is excellent advice for anyone who leads others, but especially those who answer the call to go into vocational ministry, as I did right out of college. Unfortunately, my journey to humility has been long, arduous, and is still a work in progress. Swallowing humility pills is a taste that can be difficult to acquire. Let me tell you my story beginning with a little from my childhood that will provide context for when my humility journey began as a young adult heading into college.

Growing Up

My earliest memory of wanting to be a leader is from when I was on the playground in elementary school. In my second-grade manifestation of a command-and-control and pacesetting leader, I started barking orders and telling my peers how things would be done in an elaborate playground production of Batman! When they pushed back, I distinctly remember saying, "Do what I say. Listen to me," which began many years of my trying to get others to respect me and pay attention to what I had to say. I was convinced that I was more talented than everyone else and that they just didn't understand the opportunities I offered to share with them.

Early on, I discovered musical theatre and the trumpet, both of which would be my identity throughout my childhood. I was good at both, really good, and soon, I didn't need to get people to listen to my words because my performance spoke for itself. My ego expanded as fast as my skills, and in junior high, I got to the point where I didn't care what anyone thought of me. I knew I was the best. I became overly demanding and critical of others, which caused my peers to dislike me, which resulted in my resolve to be better than everyone else hitting an all-time high. I also got to the point at which I refused to go along with anything the "crowd" did. My mantra was to see what the crowd was doing and do the opposite, and I did, every time. Junior high was a miserable time for me, but I covered up my pain by being the best in my field, but with a huge ego. At the end of the ninth grade, I got a fantastic gift. We moved to a new city where no one knew me.

High school was much better, but unfortunately, my ego moved cities with me. I was very good at what I did and everyone knew it, plus I didn't hide the fact that I knew it, too. My directors rewarded me with roles and positions and I thrived, not only in the high school setting but also community organizations, in which I was a leader and considered highly gifted and talented. Then things changed. I began to stumble into my humility journey, which would last from high school through college, marriage, career, ministry, and to this day. I tell the first part of my story because, as are many pastors in our churches, I was gifted, talented, focused, driven, and confident. I could make great things happen, which I will tell you a bit more about in a moment. The problem comes when we become so sure of ourselves that we run over people with our ambition and ego. Relationships become the casualties on our road to great achievements, even ones which are supposedly done for all the right reasons. Read on.

The Journey Began

In the latter part of high school, I got my first real taste of humble pie. I was an excellent trumpet player, having achieved first chair in every musical organization of which I was ever a part and played lead in an internationally-acclaimed group of young musicians. I was a champion, and I had my sights set on being a professional player and an award-winning band director. I auditioned for the State Honor Band, but so did a whole lot of others who were just as gifted. I didn't make it, and I was heartbroken. Awards stopped coming, and scholarships were out of my reach because, though I was very good, my competition was better. I settled on going to a small college in the middle of nowhere, where I was sure I'd be a big fish in a small pond. Unfortunately, the pond was so small that I had a miserable year and came home with my proverbial tail tucked between my legs. I transferred to a new university and started over with a better set of circumstances. Do you think that a couple of disastrous years humbled me? Unfortunately, no.

University

Although I was slightly less outwardly arrogant as I entered my new university, I was soon back to my old self again as I got back to my winning ways. I sang in the top groups, was cast in mainstage productions, and though not the best trumpet player, I was one of the best. Once again I was the one making things happen. In my junior year, several very significant things happened. First, I met my now wife of nearly four decades. It's a wonder that we lasted, because in my state of extreme confidence and cockiness, three days after we got together I let her know that we were getting married. I didn't ask, I told her, which shows you how very sure of myself I still was! Second, I felt the call to vocational ministry. I had been a Christian for a long time, but now I felt that I was supposed to spend my life in ministry. I never said this out loud, but my attitude was "How fortunate the church is to have me!"

The third thing related to the fact that I had been working for Disneyland Park in Southern California for a couple of years. I did a variety of things, but one was playing lead trumpet in a band that did a couple of parades each day. I thought it was pretty cool to do that, and it only padded my ego. Then I got the opportunity to audition for the Disney All-American College Band, which was a dream position for me. I wanted to be in that group more than anything. Although the director was complimentary of my playing, I wasn't as good as the ones who got the jobs. I was devastated, and I look to that day as when my professional trumpet-playing plans ended. It was one of the darkest times in my life up to that point. It was clear that I wasn't as good as I thought I was. Do you think that not making it into the Disney Band humbled me? Of course not.

Moving Forward

During my senior year, I stopped playing and concentrated on singing, acting (though I didn't get the roles I thought I deserved) and preparing for life as a pastor and getting married. To further demonstrate my zeal and heightened self-assurance, let me tell you a true story.

Go Right to the Top

> I was getting ready to graduate with a double degree in music and theatre arts and with the intention of going right into seminary to become a pastor. However, I knew

that God wasn't calling me to be a traditional preaching pastor, but rather to use my gifts in new and unique ways. At the time, very few churches had full-time positions for people in the arts, and the term "worship pastor" was yet to be thought up! Most churches had a part-time minister of music.

My father was a United Methodist pastor, so naturally I figured that I would attend a Methodist seminary, but I knew that I wanted something out of the ordinary. Being the confident young man that I was, I decided that I would go right to the top and make an appointment with the Bishop of the United Methodist Church. Not really to my surprise, he agreed to meet with me in his Los Angeles office. Once there I described in detail my vision for a performing arts ministry (worship arts wasn't a phrase yet) and asked him to find me a job with the denomination to do what I was the best at when I got out of seminary. He listened politely, and when I was done, he smiled and said something like, "Churches don't do that. Go to seminary, become a youth pastor, and maybe someday you can use your music."

After the meeting, I told my future wife about what he had said and she said, "Why would God gift you like He has and not expect you to use it?" We decided that day that I wasn't going to go to a Methodist seminary and that I was going to help create the kind of ministry position that I was envisioning. I was determined to prove the Bishop wrong about not only me, but also the importance of the arts in churches. Looking at what worship arts has become in the past couple of decades proves that I was right (but it would be less than humble to say so!).

⋏ ⋏ ⋏

It just so happens that at the same time as my meeting with the Bishop, I was doing an extensive research project for my degrees on the use of music and theatre in the local church. I received materials and input from dozens of publishers and I interviewed all the ministers of music who would let me in their office. One of those people was the director of the performing arts center at Robert Schuller's Garden Grove Community Church in Southern California, which was soon to become the Crystal Cathedral. The interview began with all my questions for my research, but as time passed, it changed from my interviewing him to his interviewing me. Soon afterward, I landed my first job out of college as part of the performing arts center at one of the very first megachurches (another term yet to be invented). I must admit, I was pretty pleased with myself.

Right after graduation I was working at the Crystal Cathedral, married, and very certain I was going to singlehandedly transform how the performing arts were used in churches. Remember, at the time the term "worship pastor" had not yet been invented and I was determined to blaze that trail. I spent a decade doing many great things at the church, but also working with dozens of other churches and schools on projects. I became quite a commodity. I would be in virtually a different church every day and I'd have up to six productions or projects going at once. I was thrilled to be needed and wanted, because it made me feel that I was indispensable. During that time I also discovered that I was a pretty good scriptwriter, and I began to write dramatic scripts for gospel music publishers and my own publishing company. We sold thousands of scripts over a 20-year span, and along with it, I went on the road doing workshops all over the country. I thought, "I'm finally getting what I deserve!" Do you think that this success made me humble? Sadly, no. In fact, I was fired from one church due to my egotistic attitudes, and only a one-time guest speaker at some conferences. Of course, it wasn't my fault. They obviously didn't know who I was or what I could do for them. The next few years were challenging as I had a business fail and had to deal with all the ramifications that that brought, but I kept striving. I had a mixed bag of successes and less-than-successes. Again, humility was not my modus operandi.

Worship Pastor

The next big step was to take a full-time worship pastor position at a growing and effective church. Everything seemed to go right, and before I knew it, we had a large ministry doing fantastic work, including regional events that brought in large crowds, boosted the church's stature in the area, and unfortunately, further fed my ego. I was at the top of my professional game, though I was never satisfied. However, with every success, I became more convinced of my value and indispensability. I bought the car and the house to prove to myself (and those in junior high who didn't like me) that I was somebody and that people should listen to what I had to say. Then things began to change.

God must have gotten to a point at which He had had enough of my arrogance and decided that if I was so darned cocky, He'd let me have just enough rope to hang myself. My relationships began to suffer, the good work we were doing began to have less of an impact than it once did, script sales faded, and no one seemed to want me to come and tell them of all the wonderful things they could do if they would only follow my example. Worst, I almost lost my marriage. Fortunately, somehow I put my ego aside and got into counseling, but it took a couple of counselors before one was actually able to get through to me.

During this same period of time, we were about to make a pastoral change at the church where I had been for nearly two decades, and it became clear to me that I wasn't part of the vision for the future. Convinced that I could overcome and remain valuable,

I doubled my efforts, but I was eventually cast in the role of an obstructionist and seen as rejecting the new vision for the church. The pastor, to whom I had been extremely loyal, made it clear that he was no longer in my corner. I felt adrift. I felt I had helped create a dynamic church, but I saw my role and influence completely marginalized. Do you think that this experience taught me to be humble? Actually, it started the process, even though I had a very long way to go.

Being told, though not verbally, that I was no longer needed or wanted was a huge humbling point for me. I had always counted on my natural talents to win people over, because even if my demeanor was intense and abrasive at times, the benefit that I would bring to the church was enough to get me through. I began to look for a new place to serve, and by this time I was starting to understand the concept of sacrificial service, because it would take my letting go of my desires to continue in the ministry. Although I had always intended to do what I did for the greater glory of God and to draw people to Him, my personal ambition always played into my work. I wanted God to get the eternal glory, but I wanted the earthly rewards.

A New Start

I was on the road to humility by now. Feeling that I had to leave what I had expected to be my lifelong position was terribly painful. I felt that I had been used up and discarded. My emotions were as if I had been faithful to a spouse for a lifetime, then out of the blue, got a "Dear John" letter with no possibility of reconciliation. I eventually found a church that wanted me and was looking for the kinds of things I could make happen. However, it was not as high profile as I had enjoyed in the past, and being a lifelong city boy, there was quite a culture shock when we moved to Colorado. I left my home in California much like I had done in the past, broken, and like a dog with its tail between its legs. However, even with lessons in humility all around me, I was determined to prove to certain individuals that they were wrong about me. I was angry that I had been pushed aside and incredibly hurt that I had been discarded by some to whom I had been extremely loyal. I was going to remake our life. Fortunately, through the times of humbling in the previous couple of years, my marriage had been restored. That was one of the times when God's humbling hand actually got through to me. However, had I not been willing to be humbled, this story would have had a very different turn of events. The experience of the past few years had significantly changed who I was, and although far from being truly humble, I was on the right track.

The new church was ripe and ready for me to work my "magic." I wasn't as outwardly cocky as before, so only I (and my wife) knew that I was super pleased with myself about succeeding again. This time around I was better in the humble category, but still, below the surface, I knew I had to be diligent about giving away credit to others, raising up team members, and constantly reminding my team and myself that whatever we did, it wasn't about us. My attitude about who should get the credit had really changed. Things went very well and the church benefited from a revitalized worship arts ministry. In addition, I had done some writing, was well into a successful stint as a graduate student, and had greatly improved my relationships with my wife and my children. All was good. Was I humble? A little better, but not fully.

Here We Go Again

One thing that is always the same: things change. Even in churches that resist change, it still happens when people least expect it. My role at my new church had expanded and I was well loved and cared for. I was about to enter the last year of my doctorate, I was being published, my children were happy, my marriage was great, even the dog was loving life. Then we had a pastoral change. I had been through this before, so I was determined to make this time turn out better than the last. I committed myself to be the very best team member I could possibly be so that there would be no chance that I would again be a casualty in the transition. I worked the hardest I had worked since I had arrived, taking on new responsibilities while continuing to be excellent at my current job. There was nothing I would not do for the new pastor in order to make the transition to the future a reality and overwhelming success. I was feeling pretty good about it for the first few months, then things began to happen. I found that I was being left out of discussions and that some of the things for which I had been responsible were now being placed in others' hands. As had happened before, I was marginalized so much that I became irrelevant to the future. Before too long, I was again discarded in the most painful of ways, which I won't go into here.

I left the church hurt, desperate for understanding, and with a deep sense of discouragement. Do you think that this experience has made me more humble? You bet it has.

Lessons

In the book of Isaiah, it states, "The haughtiness of man shall be humbled, and the lofty pride of men shall be brought low, and the Lord alone will be exalted in that day."[73] I cannot think of a better way to describe my story. Throughout my life, I have been blessed with talents and abilities to make things happen which made me haughty and prideful. I've enjoyed success only to eventually be consumed by my own ego and sense of privileged entitlement. God has been gracious to allow me to rebound and rebuild several times, however, my pattern has been to return to old habits, when I believed that I was the cause of the good things in my life and ministry instead of Him. I guess I am a very slow learner. It has been written that "in the ministry, few people are as full of themselves as young pastors who have achieved acclaim early."[74] That was me, but the author goes on to say, but "no one in ministry ever amounts to anything without being broken at some point."[75] That is also me: broken, but hopeful that I will remain on my humility journey and "amount" to something.

I am once again reinventing myself; however, this time around from a much more humble point of reference. I still believe that I can contribute, but I will be careful as to how I go about doing so, and especially how I feel about my own efforts and who should get the credit. In light of the seven signs of humility, which you will soon learn about, I will not be bold and stupid enough to say that I have mastered them all and have arrived at the destination of humble intelligence. However, I do believe I am on the way more than I ever have been. The events of the past year, coupled with the last few years at my previous church, have taught me an immense amount about myself and who I am in the sight of God.

My humility journey is not over. In fact, it is far from it, as I have so much more to learn and need to continue to grow in so many ways as described above. Writing this book, though, has had a tremendous impact on my own personal journey. When I began, I truly thought that I would finally get a chance to get things off my chest, but God took hold of my heart and showed me that if this book is to be helpful to others, it couldn't be about me, and that I must be willing to live out the same principles about which I am telling others. If I am to authentically suggest that others demonstrate the seven signs of the humility factor, I must do so first. The book in your hands is not the one I intended to write, but fortunately, God knew better.

There are many other pieces to my story which I have not told about which you might say, "Really, John, really?" I'm embarrassed that I have not been all that I could have been in God's service, or in my relationships, but I am making headway. As I continue on this journey, I will hold onto scripture,

> "Because your heart was tender and you humbled yourself before God when you heard his words against this place and its inhabitants, and you have humbled yourself before me and have torn your clothes and wept before me, I also have heard you," declares the Lord.[76]

I haven't actually torn my clothing, but I have shed plenty of tears. It is comforting that I can be assured that God has heard me.

Healthy churches are led by humble pastors.

CHAPTER 3

Here's How the Humility Factor Works

In this chapter we will discuss at length each of the seven attributes that make up the humility factor, but I hope that this provides a context for you as we proceed. In chapter four we will look at the wide variety of leadership styles, traits, and skills which you will find in lead pastors. As we go through these, you will most likely recognize your current or past lead pastor. It should be noted that all styles can be effective and cause a church to grow and make an impact in their community; however, not all styles lead to a church being healthy as we have defined it, which is why the humility factor matters.

You may be in the process of searching for your next lead pastor, and you are aware that there are specific issues with which your church is wrestling that will take a certain kind of leader with specific skills. Your circumstances may require an authentic servant leader with shepherding skills because your church needs healing from a difficult experience, or you may need a visionary leader because your church has become comfortable, complacent, and stuck in the status quo. This review of leadership styles and traits will help you to identify which style, traits, and skills you truly need at this point in your church's development. However, the whole point of this book is to encourage you to be on the lookout for signs of the seven attributes of the humility factor because, when applied, you will have a better leader as your next pastor.

Input from Pastor Graham Standish

Before we explore the seven attributes of the humility factor and later dive into the many styles of leadership from which you have to choose, let's take a moment to look at some examples of pastors with humble intelligence, as identified by Graham Standish himself. I've been quoting the work he's written for nearly a decade now. His book *Humble Leadership* literally changed the trajectory of my ministry, personal attitudes, and academic pursuits, and I have continued to cite his other writings as well, which include articles and many other books, so when I began this project, I made contact with him, hoping that he would respond and give me some examples of humble pastors. What I received should not have surprised me. I found out that Pastor Standish was indeed a man of humble intelligence and was personally leading a healthy church. He is the senior pastor of Calvin Presbyterian Church in Zelienople, Pennsylvania.

In his response to me, he said,

> One reason I wrote the book was my sense of the dearth of humility among pastors. I've found that many are somewhat arrogant to one degree or another (often theologically arrogant, thinking they are right about things – others administratively arrogant, thinking that only they know what's wrong with the church and what it needs to do). Others are sort of humiliated by what they see as their failures.

THE HUMILITY FACTOR

As I read that, I said, "Wow. That's exactly what I'm talking about." Pastor Standish had his finger on the pulse of the problem that holds many churches hostage to becoming healthy. Their pastors lack the humble intelligence which comes from the humility factor.

I asked Pastor Standish if he could identify pastors whom he considered to be humble. I subsequently connected with each one and here are pieces of some of their stories. It should be noted that in every case, they began their response to me with a disclaimer as to how surprised they were that they were considered to be humble! This alone was an awesome confirmation that they were the right people with whom I should speak about pastoral humility.

Pastor Paul Hoffman served as the pastor of Phinney Ridge Lutheran Church in Seattle, WA, until he retired in 2013. I am including most of his response because it lends considerable support to my premise that healthy churches are led by humble pastors. Make sure to note his opening statement.

> Wow. I do not believe that many people who know me well would consider me humble. I think they would tend to use words like: driven, self-assured, determined, maybe even arrogant. So your e-mail takes me by surprise. For whatever way I can contribute, here are some things that I would say about parish leadership (from which, incidentally, I am now retired) that may be helpful.
>
> Above all, I believe that an effective pastor has to be willing to be a servant-leader. That is to say, in the briefest possible way, you cannot be above setting up tables and chairs in the fellowship hall. Your people have to know that you care deeply about them and that you will be there for them. When a man with Alzheimer's disease is dying at 2 a.m. and his soon-to-be widow calls,

your response <u>must</u> be, "I will be there as soon as I can," not, "Please let me know when I'm in the office at 9 how John is doing." If you exhibit the sort of humility that says, "I am here to serve you," then I believe your ministry will flourish. That does not mean that they own you, or can walk all over you. It simply means that if you demonstrate from day one that you believe you are CALLED to be their pastor and SERVE them, it will cover a multitude of sins, even some of my self-perceived character flaws listed above.

I also believe that my own humble beginnings with parents who dearly loved the Lord and Christ's church but were dirt-poor farmers taught me a great deal about the human condition. One who wishes to serve well cannot be afraid to get one's hands dirty with the real events of life: birth, death, illness, humiliation, madness. Luther put it this way, at least anecdotally: *No one should be called to ministry until they have smelled the fart of an old sow.* Growing up on a farm and witnessing the cycles of nature – seed time and harvest; conception, birth, growth, death gives one a particular lens into life that I believe served me well as a pastor.

Another humble characteristic is the ability to pray openly, freely, and often with one's congregation – individually and collectively. To pray *sincerely* and attentively. In preaching, I think it is always important and a sign of humility to use the pronouns "we" and "I." Those who preach to "you" are most often not taken seriously. I have cherished the opportunities to say homiletically, "I don't know if it is the case for you, but I find that sin lurks at every complicated intersection of my life..."

⟁ ⟁ ⟁

Phinney Ridge is a part of the Evangelical Lutheran Churches of America and is a mix of traditional liturgical worship and progressive social consciousness. A quick look at their website makes it obvious that the church is healthy and vibrant, meeting the needs of a diverse congregation. One of the best ways to know who they are and what they value comes from the statement they make on their home page, which states,

> As people made one in the waters of baptism, we believe our lives and faith are strengthened by diversity. We strive to be a community that welcomes people of every ability, age, citizenship status, ethnicity, gender identity and expression, language, life circumstance, marital status, political perspective, race, and sexual orientation. Whether you are a believer, doubter, or seeker, we openly welcome and value you. We celebrate God's unconditional love and respond joyfully to your presence here. All are welcome. You are welcome.[77]

Though Pastor Hoffman is no longer the senior pastor, his fingerprints are still evident in every aspect of the church's approach to fulfilling their calling to Christ and being a healthy and humble church.

The next example Dr. Standish offered is Pastor Steve Jacobsen, who led the Goleta Presbyterian Church in Goleta, CA, for 27 years before taking the helm of La Casa de Maria Retreat Center on the coast of California, where their purpose is "to be a sanctuary of peace." When I spoke with him and asked him to name the three to five most important characteristics a pastor should have, he listed humility, the ability to genuinely listen to God, and someone who likes people. He shared how Jesus spent 85% of his time not in the church (temple), but out with the people, and that one of the major problems churches have today is that there is too much gap between the church and real people. Churches and their leaders can be impractical and inauthentic. He also pointed out that when Jesus got angry, it was often with those who were self-righteous, such as the Pharisees of the temple. Jesus' words "Woe to you" made it clear that church leaders should be genuinely humble. Pastor Jacobsen told me that "humility makes room for others," and I loved his additional statement that expressed how humble leaders should interact with people: "Make compost, not roses."

Today the Goleta church built by Pastor Jacobsen remains healthy, active, and deeply committed to children, youth, worship, and particularly local and global missions. They do so even while still in the process of seeking their next long-term pastor. They are currently led by a transitional pastor supplied by the denomination; however, they do not appear to have missed a beat.

Another example of a humble pastor identified by Pastor Standish is Bishop Young Jin Cho, who served as the bishop of the Virginia United Methodist Church Conference from 2012 to 2016 following leading one of its local churches. As was the pattern with these pastors, his first words to me were, "I am not sure I am the right person you are looking for." As I have read through the considerable amount of information I have on Bishop Cho, I am struck by his words,

> Greatness of life is not in being served, but in serving. We are not in charge. Jesus is in charge. Ministry is not my ministry or our ministry, but Christ's ministry. The Risen Christ is still alive and doing His ministry in us and among us through the Holy Spirit. Mission is not my mission or our mission. We are taking part in God's mission. If we humbly open ourselves and seek and obey the will of our Lord, we will have a different future.

Then there was Rev. Leon Johnston of Wolf Creek Community Church in Lacombe, Alberta, Canada, who responded,

> Two things come to mind. The first is listening. A humble leader is willing to listen to people, whether it be a neighbor, a child, or another leader, etc. A humble leader also listens to God through his word and by spending time with Him through solitude and silence. And that brings me to my second point. A humble leader is a man/woman of prayer. But I'm not sure how much we as leaders focus on prayer, as it doesn't necessarily "please" the people, although it is desperately needed.

Wolf Creek is an active and healthy church, though very unassuming at first glance. Their website states, "We are a group of people whose lives and whose stories are being transformed by the love of God," and they make a point of telling people that their aim is to be hospitable to everyone. Rev. Leon is a younger pastor with a great vision, but well in touch with the diverse makeup of his congregation.

All of the above pastors are just some of the ones highlighted in this book for possessing humble intelligence as a result of the humility factor in the way they serve in ministry. Interesting observations of the pastors identified by Pastor Standish are that each represents what are considered "mainline" churches, and two are located in Canada, which makes it clear that humility is a universal quality necessary for all people and all denominations.

What is Humility? What Does it Look Like? How Did Jesus Model it?

My friend, and author of the book *Eats With Sinners*, Pastor Arron Chambers, put the concept of being a humble pastor in perspective when he states, "As we eat with sinners, it would be wise to start each meal with a slice of humble pie. If we really want to reach lost people, we must be humble – and true humility comes from standing next to the cross."[78] I can think of no greater way to keep our outlook on leadership humble than by seeing everything that we do through the comparative lens of Jesus, who had everything, but set it all aside for the sole purpose of reestablishing a connection between His Heavenly Father and the human race, which is why He is the ultimate example whom pastors should emulate when leading a church. Ethicist and theologian Kyle Fedler states, "An important thing to remember when evaluating if someone is suitable for leadership is Christ's example. Jesus is the embodiment and fulfillment of what God intended you and me to be."[79] In every way Jesus showed us how pastors should conduct themselves. We must keep His practices in mind, though they are the opposite of how most leaders, particularly in the marketplace, are expected to behave. "In every possible way," states Dr. Gary Oster, the author of *The Light Prize*, "Jesus disrupted the status quo."[80]

Our culture expects and even encourages leaders to do everything they can with their own best interest in mind. That is the way most leaders believe they will be successful as the one in charge, or as the "first chair," so to speak. Bonem and Patterson discuss how "second chair" leaders are to relate to their superiors, which is a good analogy for pastors to keep in mind, because in the spiritual hierarchy of church leadership, the first chair should belong to God and the second chair to either a pastor or a group of pastors collaboratively. Bonem and Patterson also discuss the paradox of being both a leader and a subordinate simultaneously. Second chair leaders (pastors) must be content to follow the first chair (God) while continuing to dream about their future and leading others.[81] Theologian and scholar Corne' J. Bekker describes this type of humble pastoral leader as one who leads "with a calm and quiet determination to make a difference in their world, without the encumbrance of public adulation or selfish ambition."[82] They do as scripture teaches in Psalm 25:9, allow themselves to be led by God, who "leads the humble in what is right and teaches the humble his way,"[83] knowing that as James 4:20 states, when people "humble themselves before the Lord, they will be exalted."[84]

This does not suggest that a humble pastor should be weak in their leadership abilities in any way. In fact, churches need pastors who are gifted and confident in the use of their skills. Keucher reminds us that humility in a pastor is "neither genuine nor feigned self-abasement, but an appropriate, accurate estimate of one's abilities and accomplishments."[85] Humility, by definition, "involves an accurate or moderate view of one's strengths and weaknesses as well as being interpersonally other-oriented rather than self-focused, marked by the ability to restrain egotism in ways that maintain social acceptance."[86] All of these concepts will be covered in the seven signs of the humility factor.

Before moving on to describe these seven signs and what church lay leaders should look for in a pastoral candidate, I want to point out how previous research corroborates this study of humble pastoral leaders. I borrow further from the research of Dr. Corne' J. Bekker, who asked if leaders could truly be humble. His affirmative position included citing the work of organizational guru Jim Collins and the words of a sixth-century monk, St. Benedict of Nursia. To this I will add another saint, though a modern uncanonized individual who would most likely be quite uncomfortable with the title, lawyer-turned-philanthropist Bob Goff. Below you will see the similarities between Dr. Bekker's findings and the humility factor.

Citing a 2001 *Harvard Business Review* article by Collins, Dr. Bekker lists the following:

- Personally humble leaders demonstrate a compelling modesty. They shun public adulation and never boast.
- Personally humble leaders act with calm and quiet determination, not relying on inspiring charisma to motivate, but rather inspired standards.
- Personally humble leaders avoid personal ambition in favor of multi-generational organizational growth and development.
- Personally humble leaders are self-reflective and tend to appropriate blame towards themselves and not others.[87]

Following a similar tone, St. Benedict of Nursia lists twelve steps to humility:

- Respect God
- Love not your own will
- Submit to your leader
- Be steadfast
- Be transparent
- Be content with your job
- See yourself correctly
- Stay within boundaries
- Control your tongue
- Avoid mindless frivolity
- Speak plainly and clearly
- Have a humble posture[88]

The following statement from Bob Goff simply serves as a reminder that when churches look for their leaders, they mustn't feel required to look for a rock star, but rather a humble servant. He states,

> I reflect on God, who didn't choose someone else to express His creative presence to the world, who didn't tap the rock star or the popular kid to get things done. He chose you and me. We are the means, the method, the object, and the delivery vehicles. God can use anyone, for sure. If you can shred on a Fender or won '"Best Personality," you're not disqualified – it just doesn't make you *more* qualified. You see, God usually chooses ordinary people like us to get things done.[89]

Well said, Bob. You may not see yourself as a saint, but there are many who know the work that you humbly do around the world who would vote sainthood upon you!

Bob is an example of how humble people can participate in God's work in extraordinary ways, as he is someone who doesn't just talk about doing good work, but actually does it. Pastor Doug Hall, the author of The Cat and the Toaster, calls this "doing the Bible,"[90] meaning that people of today can have just as much impact for the cause of Christ as the people we read about in scripture. Churches need pastors, who, like Pastor Hall and Bob Goff, "do the Bible" and understand that they are called to make a contribution that is a consistent vision of love and one that creates within the community in which they live a culture of compassion,[91] which just happens to be the first sign of the humility factor.

Seven Signs of the Humility Factor
There have been scores of self-help books published over the past century that preach the importance of individuals and organizations

developing the correct habits in order to achieve the results they desire. There is no less importance placed here on the habits of a lead pastor who has attained humble intelligence. The following seven signs, or attributes, of the humility factor should be habitual on the part of the pastor and should be quite evident when you are combing through the stack of resumes you receive when you are looking for a new pastor for your church. More so, these should be obvious in the person you choose to interview face to face.

Remember, healthy churches are led by humble pastors, and when the humility factor is added to any style of leadership someone possesses, leadership will improve. You will get a crash course in leadership styles in the next chapter to help you identify the kind of leader that you believe your church needs right now, but I strongly urge you to make sure that you are also actively looking for the evidence of these seven signs of the humility factor. You may find a potential lead pastor who has the leadership chops, but if you can find one with the same skills plus the humility factor, you will be miles ahead on your journey to becoming a truly healthy church. Make sure that you don't just see traces of the signs that may be put on just for the interviewing process. You want to look for evidence that the humility factor is a habit, which can be seen from a broader and longer-term perspective. Humble leaders usually don't start out humble. It requires life experiences that mold them into a humble vessel that God can use to lead your church. Take your time and really dig deep to find the humility factor. In describing each of the seven signs, I will provide a thorough description of what to look for, a pastor that displays these traits, and how Jesus modeled them. Remember, what we are seeking is a pastor who displays the sum of the seven attributes of the humility factor (HF) humble intelligence (HI), then adds it to their leadership style (L) to result in a humble pastor (HP), as illustrated in the following model.

$$\text{Sum of HF = HI} + \text{L} = \text{HP}$$

Compassion

The first of the seven signs to look for in a potential lead pastor is compassion, evidenced by the behaviors of empathy, grace, and especially love. While all of the seven signs are important attributes of the humility factor, compassion rises to the top of desired traits for pastors, because when they show compassion for people within the church and for others in the community and around the world, they display an important trait of Jesus Christ. One of the things which many people who have become turned off to church point to as to why they are distrustful of churches, church people, and their pastors is that churches often talk of love and taking care of others, but don't back up their rhetoric with action, or their words don't match how they actually treat others. Bickel and Jantz, authors of *I'm Fine with God...It's Christians I Can't Stand*, document many non-churchgoers who believe this and state, "Christians don't need to revamp the culture in order to regain respect in society. We simply need to start conducting ourselves in the loving manner that Christ intended all along."[92] Pastor Tony Campolo states, "The biggest problem Christians face in their involvement with politics is that politics is about power, while being Christian is about love."[93] Compassion, when shown through empathy, grace, and true love, is not only how a pastor can share in the example set by Christ, but also demonstrate their humble intelligence.

Compassion, in its truest form, "cares for the other person more than one's self and seeks the welfare of others."[94]

Empathy
Similar to humble intelligence, emotional intelligence makes a strong case for the critical trait of empathy by a leader, which manifests itself in a leader's ability to listen, understand, and come alongside one of their followers as they struggle with a dilemma or challenge in their life. Pastors, particularly in churches that have a smaller staff, are often expected to be not only a Bible scholar, administrator, and dynamic communicator, but also a marriage counselor and life coach for members of their congregation. They must be able to show that they care about their flock. One of the greatest examples of Jesus' showing empathy is when, even though He knew that He would soon raise Lazarus from the dead, He wept along with Mary and Martha for the loss of their brother.[95] Some pastors are naturally gifted in this way, as we will discuss in the next chapter when describing a shepherd-style pastor, but even if this is not a natural gift, pastors with humble intelligence have the ability to show compassion through empathy. The apostle Paul said it this way, "Bear one another's burdens, and in this way you will fulfill the law of Christ."[96]

Grace
Another way a pastor shows compassion is through giving grace as Jesus did, not only to the people with whom He came in contact, but ultimately to all who would accept Him as Savior. Without grace, Christianity would not exist and your church would not exist. It was through grace that everything we believe came into being. I recently heard Pastor Curt Harlow of Bayside Church state, "Grace is everything for nothing to those who don't deserve

anything." The people before Jesus made His appearance on earth were bound and burdened by the law and the never-ending requirements that were placed on them by the religious leaders, which were virtually impossible to achieve. It was only by the grace of God, through Jesus' death on the cross, that we were freed from a standard that kept us in bondage. God showed His compassion through the grace and mercy He poured out on all who would believe. Jesus demonstrated the kind of grace a pastor must show to his team when he met with Peter after His resurrection and restored him to ministry, even though Peter had denied knowing Him.[97]

Pastors must have the same mindset as God when it comes to grace. They are to teach laws and standards, inspire people to follow, and gently reprimand those who make poor or disastrous decisions, but they should at no time withhold the same amount of grace which God has given to everyone. They are to guide people to the right path, but judgment and exile from the fellowship of believers are in God's hands, and far above a pastor's pay grade. Here is a little bit of my story that demonstrates this.

Artists! Arg!

> I served as a worship pastor for 25 years, so I had the wonderful privilege of leading and shepherding many wonderful servants of God in the church. The people I led were passionate, gifted, energetic, and committed. They blessed the people they led in the worship of the Most High God, and me as well. They were also artists, which means that passion and emotion usually run deep, which is a wonderful thing. However, sometimes it can get people into trouble because the devil loves to mess with them. I've said countless times that the people leading others in

worship and doing things to bring people to a relationship with Christ have a huge target on their back. The devil will do whatever he can to mess with the worship ministry of a church. Sometimes their emotions and passion get the best of them and they make poor choices, with which I've had to deal on a pastoral level.

I'm happy to say that there were very few times where I wasn't able to get people's attention, help them see things in the way God would want them to, and restore them to the place where they joyfully served God and the church with the right spirit and behaviors. It has never been easy, but my secret weapon in dealing with these challenges is grace. I always err on the side of showing grace, even when people are making really dumb decisions. I do this not only because I see Jesus' model, but because I have been someone who has needed a lot of grace shown to me. If I had not, I would not be in the ministry today, and I would not have been privileged to serve the many people in the churches in which God allowed me a place on the team, and certainly, I would not be writing this book! Grace was needed for me big time, so I am always quick to give it to others, even if they are still doing things which they know better than to do. I have many excellent stories, which will remain confidential, of people who made some really bad choices, but I was able to help them deal with the consequences and get them back on the right road, which allows them to be a part of God's work to this day. Sometimes I've been criticized for showing too much grace too quickly, but I wouldn't change a thing as I picture each person whom God is using today for His glory through His grace.

Love

The final part of the sign of the humility factor of compassion is love, a principle of true biblical humility, which Jesus modeled in every way possible. All of Christ's actions were prompted by His deep love for the people, which He taught and showed to the very end.[98] The basic phrase, "Love your neighbor as yourself," can be found in a variety of places in the Bible, going back to Leviticus 19:18; through the gospels of Matthew, Mark, and Luke; and in the writings of Paul in Galatians and James in his book. In the account from Matthew, Jesus is speaking with the religious leaders whose intent was to lure Him into saying things with which they could find fault to turn the crowd against Him. One of the Pharisaic lawyers attempted to trap Jesus with his question about which commandment was the greatest, a question often debated by the Pharisees and Sadducees. According to Matthew Henry's commentary, the question was not intended to question Jesus' knowledge, but rather His judgment.[99]

Jesus' response, which combined two commandments into one complete unit,[100] was quite revolutionary, and represented a redefinition of the manifestation of the love of God, man's obligation to love others, and whom the recipients should be.[101] Our first love must be for God with our whole being, but then for others, shown by doing everything possible in all circumstances as we would wish others to do for us, because our neighbor is in the image and likeness of God found in all people and, according to Gill's *Exposition,* "Love is due every man."[102] When Jesus said, "Love your neighbor as yourself,"[103] He placed value on all people and expected His followers to treat others as they would desire to be treated themselves. It is both an ethical and compassionate responsibility to think and act in special ways in all circumstances,[104] explicitly commanded by Christ and fulfilled by obeying the will of God, which is to love your neighbor as yourself.[105]

People want and need to know that their leader cares about what is going on in their lives and trust that the leader is looking out for their well-being as well as others'. Often compassion is as simple as the leader's remembering that the church decisions that are made and how they are implemented will have a lasting effect on the individual lives of the people who make up the church, as they are not disposable or mere parts of a machine that can be discarded without harm being done. Sometimes compassion is shown on a broader scale as a pastor initiates community- or worldwide efforts to make people's lives better.

Jesus said, "Love your neighbor as yourself," and with it comes the implied responsibility of doing so in the way that He would do. It's not an option. How we treat others is a reflection of how we love God. It can't be forced and it can't be phony. Love must be genuine because it "rejoices with the truth."[106] Above all, love is our calling as Christian leaders. As N. T. Wright described, we must not think of love as our duty, but rather, our destiny.[107] The same is true for compassion, which you will see in the next example of a church making compassion a priority, and more important, a reality.

When What a Church Says Matches What They Do

One of the churches to which I often point as an example of being successful, effective, and healthy is Bayside Church in Granite Bay, CA. Its founding pastor is Ray Johnston, and he is an outstanding example of compassion. Ray describes how he was introduced to Compassion International by someone sitting next to him on a flight whose job it was to audit relief agencies. Somewhat skeptical about the claims he had heard, he looked them up and became intrigued. Then he was invited to visit and thoroughly check it out. It is a global ministry organization that arranges for people to sponsor children in countries in which they had little hope of breaking out of the cycle of poverty common to much of the population. Their mission statement is "Releasing children from poverty in Jesus' name," which resonated with Ray, as he believes that "Whoever wins the kids wins the culture. Whoever wins the kids wins the nation. Whoever wins the kids ultimately wins."[108]

Upon further investigation, Ray was hooked, and he has become a huge advocate for Compassion International. By 2014, Bayside had already sponsored 8000 children, with the numbers constantly growing, as the Compassion International cause has become a major mission for Ray, his staff, and all of the Bayside campuses. One cannot attend services for very long, or go to a concert, event, or conference, without having the opportunity to sponsor a child. "Releasing compassion" has even become one of Bayside's core statements of how they conduct ministry, and it doesn't stop with the international focus. It is evident in everything the church does on a local level, from "serve days," when they shut down all services to send the congregation out into the community to serve people in countless ways, to bringing relief when tragedy strikes a family or a community, to raising thousands of dollars for a tip for a pizza delivery driver going through challenging times. Releasing compassion is not just a slogan for Bayside; it is what they actually do.

⸭ ⸭ ⸭

The conclusion, then, is that the building block for leaders who choose to love their neighbors as themselves is compassion, through a natural sympathy and a concern for the well-being of others.[109] The author of *Authentic Leadership*, Bill George, raises the question as to whether a person can be an authentic leader without compassion. He answers, "Not really, although some leaders behave as though they have no compassion for anyone."[110] I would agree, and add that one cannot be a humble leader without it.

> **Healthy churches are led by humble pastors. Humble pastors have humble intelligence through the humility factor, which includes compassion as observed in empathy, grace, and love.**

The Humility Factor in Action

At the end of each description of the seven signs are helpful questions to ask and what to look for when interviewing a potential pastor and when evaluating your current pastor.

Questions to Ask and What to Look For:

1. Does the pastoral candidate show signs of empathy by being genuinely interested in and caring about the people they serve?
2. Are they good listeners?
3. Do they exhibit grace when dealing with people who have made poor choices?
4. Are they willing to walk alongside someone to restore them to ministry and fellowship?
5. Do they follow Jesus' command to "love thy neighbor?"
6. Do they show love and care to others in practical ways without bias or preference?

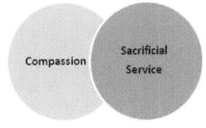

Sacrificial Service

The second sign to look for in a potential lead pastor is sacrificial service, which can be simply described as the willingness to do something for others which will require a personal sacrifice of some kind. It might be the sacrifice of time, money, position, recognition, comfort, or something else, any of which lessens one's own status or condition of life. Many authors have written scores of books and articles on the subject of sacrifice and service. Many have a convicting, though unintentional, tone that causes the reader to step back and take stock of one's life and priorities.

Modern writer Christena Cleveland makes such a statement when she writes, "If you don't have to give up power, then it's not really servant leadership."[111] Her point is that when there is no change in the power difference between the leader and the follower, calling oneself a servant leader isn't truly accurate. One must actually sacrifice something in service to the other, just as Jesus did when He gave up His power to command all of heaven to come to His aid, and allowed the power to be in the hands of those He came to serve.

Twentieth-century writer Francis Schaeffer writes even stronger words of warning when defining a pastor's spirituality before God. He described lives with the attachments to material possessions with which many Christians tend to live as "ash heap lives" and said that human materialism is a sign that personal possession, personal pride, and personal gain have distracted leaders from seeing God clearly.[112] It's rare that a pastor who has achieved the status of a celebrity Christian leader will walk away from it in favor of God's calling to sacrificial service, but that is exactly what happened in the next story.

Too Much Francis Chan

An excellent example of this level of sacrificial service is pastor/author Francis Chan, who, at the height of his ministry in 2010, abruptly resigned as pastor of a growing 4000-member church in Southern California and left the country. It may be tempting to ask, "What really happened that caused him to give it all up?" However, it was reported that "there was apparently no hidden scandal, no money trail, and no 'other' woman."[113] Chan states, "Even in my own church I heard the words, 'Francis Chan' more than I heard the words, 'Holy Spirit.' I think there has been too much emphasis on me. I want to be used of God, but I think we have this desire to make heroes out of people rather than following God and the Holy Spirit."[114] Chan left the church, country, and internet so that he could sacrificially serve others one on one.

▲ ▲ ▲

Francis Chan's case is radical, and some may say extreme, but it demonstrates the concept of being willing to give up things which bring one power and prestige in favor of being the hands and feet of Jesus to people who cannot give anything in return. Today Chan has returned to the U.S. and is a popular speaker at conferences and as a guest preacher, but I would speculate that he would disappear into the wilderness again if God called him to do so.

Of course, no discussion of sacrificial service can leave out the well-known theologian Vince Lombardi. He is quoted to have said, "Leadership is in sacrifice, it is in self-denial, it is in love and loyalty, it is in fearlessness, it is in humility, and it is in the perfectly disciplined will. This is the distinction between great and little men."[115] I would venture to say that the example set by Pastor Chan fits Coach Lombardi's description in every way, as does Jesus, who, "even as the Son of Man came not to be served but to serve, and to give his life as a ransom for many."[116] Jesus was God, yet He still chose to sacrifice all He was in order to serve the greater purposes of His Heavenly Father. What a radical concept! Sanders, in the book *Spiritual Leadership*, states,

> Jesus was a revolutionary, not in the guerrilla warfare sense but in His teaching on leadership. He overturned an existing order. In the world's ears, the term servant spoke everywhere of low prestige, low respect, low honor. Most people were not attracted to such a low-value role. When Jesus used the term, however, it was a synonym for greatness. And that was a revolutionary idea. It still is!

As churches are searching for their next lead pastor, they need to look for a pastor who will emulate the example Jesus set. Of course you may want someone immensely talented who will be able to set the church on a clear trajectory to new heights, but without the humility factor attribute of sacrificial service, you may end up with a pastor who is more concerned with becoming a famous pastor who writes books, travels the world speaking, and is a Christian household name, just like Francis Chan before he gave it all up to spend his time preaching to small churches in the forgotten villages of Asia.

There are many examples of Jesus living out sacrificial service, but few as famous as when He washed the feet of His disciples on the eve of His arrest as a servant would do.

> Jesus, knowing that the Father had given all things into his hands, and that he had come from God and was going back to God, rose from supper. He laid aside his outer

garments, and taking a towel, tied it around his waist. Then he poured water into a basin and began to wash the disciples' feet and to wipe them with the towel that was wrapped around him.[117]

Pastor Wayne Cordeiro of New Hope Church in Honolulu states this regarding the need for pastors to be servants:

> Let us consider the heart of a servant. Regardless of a person's gifts, talents, or abilities, each of us is called to the foot of the table. At New Hope we say, "The fastest way to the throne will always be through the servant's entrance." Whatever the need is, we need to be willing to pick up a towel and wash someone's feet.[118]

Picking up the towel of Jesus is not easy. It requires a total sacrifice of what most leaders are led to believe leaders are. Sacrificial service is the antithesis of power, prestige, ambition, and personal gain, but it is a critical piece of the humility factor. In the book *Leaders Eat Last*, Simon Sinek states,

> Leaders are the ones willing to look out for those to the left of them and those to the right of them. They are often willing to sacrifice their own comfort for ours, even when they disagree with us. Leaders are the ones who are willing to give up something of their own for us. Their time, their energy, their money, maybe even the food off their plate. When it matters, leaders choose to eat last.[119]

Not only last, but often in secret. Bob Goff speaks of sacrificial service as being "more like sign language than being spoken outright."[120] He challenges us to stop talking about what we will do and just "go do stuff"[121] – not to direct attention to one's self, but "toward an approachable God."[122] Fame may not come to the secretly sacrificial servant, but God knows what has been done and will always find a way to make things work out for the humble and sacrificial servant in the end.[123] As Jesus taught,

> Beware of practicing your righteousness before other people in order to be seen by them, for you will have no reward from your Father who is in heaven. When you give to the needy, do not let your left hand know what your right hand is doing, so that your giving may be in secret. And your Father who sees in secret will reward you.[124]

Healthy churches are led by humble pastors. Humble pastors have humble intelligence through the humility factor, which includes sacrificial service.

The Humility Factor in Action
Questions to Ask and What to Look For:

1. Are they willing to put their own needs aside in order to meet the needs of others?
2. Do they seek recognition and rewards for their service?
3. Are they willing to do whatever needs to get done without feeling that some things are below them?

Openness

The third attribute that makes up the humility factor is openness. Basically, how open will your pastor be to learning new things, listening to and including others, and following the leading of the Holy Spirit? If they believe that they already have all the answers and don't need any further input, they do not have humble intelligence, and you should look elsewhere. If you've already hired someone who is convinced of their infallibility, you need to do some serious work to help them become more open.

Open to Learning

I'm not the only author speaking about the need for healthy churches. Recently Pete Scazzero of *Outreach Magazine* spoke of the importance of pastors being lifetime learners who are humble, curious, and teachable.[125] It's a sad commentary that so many articles have been written on the need for organizations to become learning organizations and for their leaders to remain open-minded to new thoughts, practices, and shifts in long-standing paradigms. Open-mindedness is on the list of "great leader qualities" recently published by *Entrepreneur Magazine*,[126] which states the obvious, but often missed, point that if a leader stops being open to new ideas, they begin a slow march to the irrelevancy of their organization, or worse, its demise. The same is true for churches, as they must continue to adapt and be agile when it comes to the methods and practices for reaching modern culture.

All too often, pastors will decide what it takes to do ministry, then literally "close their mental notebook" to learning.[127] They become, as one writer identifies, "Dukes of Habit who must always do things the same way, must have everything in its place, and are at a loss if something violates their routines."[128] When this happens, effectiveness stalls and the church falls into a state of status quo, in which effort and energy are focused on hanging on to what they have, rather than discovering what they could become. When assessing the openness of a pastor, it is crucial to evaluate and reward for learning capacity,[129] rather than mere current performance, as results will fade without investment, just as a beautiful plant will wither and die without water and tending.

The following statement made by British Petroleum CEO John Brown in 2000 about organizations can be applied to churches and their pastors.

> Learning is at the heart of a company's ability to adapt to a rapidly changing environment. It is the key to being able both to identify opportunities that others might not see and to exploit those opportunities rapidly and fully. This means that in order to generate extraordinary value, a company has to learn better than its competitors and apply knowledge throughout its businesses faster and more widely than they do.[130]

Jesus modeled this quality of being open to learning in that prior to his ministry he went through the formal rabbinical training that took most of two decades. By the time he was teaching the multitudes, he had done the hard work of learning the scriptures and earning the title of "Rabbi," which even members of the Pharisees used when addressing him.[131]

Open to Others

How does your pastor, or how will your future pastor, respond when a member of the board or a congregation member makes a suggestion? Will they smile, listen, and consider what is being said, or will they get angry and insulted because they are convinced they know what's best? Will they think "How dare they tell me how to do my job? Don't they know who I am?" The latter is definitely not the kind of leader you want running your church. Instead, you want a leader with humble intelligence who is open to hearing the views of others, even if they are contrary to the direction of the church and the vision the pastor has worked hard to communicate. David Setran of Wheaton College quotes 17th century pastor Richard Baxter, who discusses this kind of prideful minister as "always teaching but unwilling to learn from others" because he has "a sense that their own words are always of greater importance than others and he is full of himself."[132]

When it is evident that a leader thinks their ideas are always better than others', the people around them tire of the arrogance and pull back in their commitment and loyalty because of the apparent artificiality of the pastor.[133] In contrast, authentic and humble pastors welcome the input of others. They not only are open to it when they are approached, but they seek it out. They welcome dialogue. The next story demonstrates how harmful it can be when people feel that their voice is pointless and disregarded.

A Royal Waste of Time

> There was a new pastor who proclaimed to the staff that they were going to function as a collaborative team. Discussion would always be conducted regarding practices, policies, events, activities, programming, and anything that concerned the church. The statement made repeatedly was "The best idea wins." This was all well and good, and a significant change in procedure from the previous pastor. The staff liked the idea and had a sense of optimism about how they would be involved in the future

decision-making for the church. "The best idea wins" sounded like the perfect way to move the church forward, beginning with a positive environment among the staff, which the new leader appeared to be fully committed to; however, unfortunately, the zealous new pastor believed that he always had the best idea. He would open things up for discussion, but soon into the process, it became clear that he had already decided the direction the church would take, and he was simply waiting for everyone else to get on board.

This was observed a number of times, but there is no better example than when, in the first couple of months of his tenure, he assembled a group of hand-picked, high-quality, and highly-committed church volunteer leaders for an intense two-day session to develop and set in motion a new vision for the church. The workshop was led by a qualified consultant, and over the two days, the group produced a well-thought-through and thoroughly-discussed set of priorities which they felt were of utmost importance for the church which the new pastor had just inherited. The feeling in the room was upbeat, optimistic, and satisfied with the work they had done.

During the last of the sessions, though, the new pastor and the consultant, who was obviously in on the pastor's plan, basically pulled a bait and switch on an organizational level. The priorities that the group had spent two days developing were discounted and replaced with a set that had obviously been developed by the pastor prior to the meeting. Instead of proceeding with what this group had labored over, another plan was announced. Afterwards, many of the members wondered why they had gone through the exercise at all. Others were insulted that their input and priorities had been discounted and dismissed.

Unfortunately, the pastor's pattern of acting like he was listening but then disrespecting the viewpoints of others in favor of his own continued, making it unclear if the best ideas, in fact, ever won, because others' ideas weren't given a chance.

▲ ▲ ▲

Unfortunately the preceding story was not the only time this pastor acted in this way. With both the staff and the board, he often spoke of how he wanted decisions to be collaborative and that he was truly open to the idea of others, only to get to the end of the process and present the way that he had already decided was the best way to go. People expect dominant leaders to have their plans laid out with the expectation of everyone falling in line and carrying out the orders; however, when a pastor loudly proclaims that they are a collaborator and that the "best idea will win," then disregards the input of others in favor of their predetermined agenda, people lose trust, commitment erodes, morale fades, and people just stop talking. They may stick around because they like the outcomes, but they will be very cautious about speaking up in the future because, in their minds, "What's the point? He's going to do things the way he wants anyway."

In God's work, agendas must begin and end with Him, but also be a collaborative process bringing together the best ideas of everyone.[134] I do not believe that there is any leader, pastor or other person who always has the best idea. Ron Edmonson states, "Humble leaders initiate others' suggestions and feedback, not waiting until complaints come, but personally asking for the input."[135] Humble leaders understand that they are not the only ones with knowledge, understanding and God-given inspiration.[136] They work at daily improvement[137] towards the goal of humble intelligence, in which inquiry and learning become the operational norm.[138]

Scripture states, "The way of a fool is right in his own eyes, but a wise man listens to advice."[139] In other words, learning, being willing to learn, and learning how to learn matter greatly if one is to take a humble approach to leading a church. Relying only on what one already believes is the way of the fool, but opening one's mind to learn about other viewpoints makes one wise. Leaders must learn all they can by intentionally being open and seeing life through other people's eyes,[140] thus opening lines of communication which can lead to understanding, empathy, partnership, mutual respect, and collective effort for the common good.[141]

Open to the Holy Spirit

The last evidence of openness on the part of a pastor is what Pastor Standish described as Spirit-active leadership, in which "it is leadership that proactively considers all possibilities, yet that does so by placing them before God in prayer. At its root is humble leadership because it seeks God's way over our own way."[142] As congregational members, we need to be assured that the leaders of our churches are listening to a greater power rather than depending on their own ingenuity, cleverness, or preference. They must be open to God's plan over their plan, or even the congregation's plan. God may have an entirely different path He wants a church to take, so we must have pastors who are willing to put their personal agendas aside in favor of God's agenda. Scazzero warned that pastors of healthy churches must not rush, because decisions that are made too quickly, without pausing to pray, think, and process implications, almost always result in regret. A leader may see the promised land, but without carefully discerning God's timing and direction, detours and painful disciplining from God can occur.[143]

Jesus modeled the way for us in being open to the Holy Spirit by the many accounts we have of them together such as at Jesus' baptism, "He went up from the water, and behold, the heavens were opened to him, and he saw the Spirit of God descending like a dove and coming to rest on him"[144]; in the desert, "And Jesus, full of the Holy Spirit, returned from the Jordan and was led by the Spirit in the wilderness"[145]; in Acts, "And God anointed Jesus of Nazareth with the Holy Spirit and with power"[146]; and in the ancient proclamation made by the prophet Isaiah, who said, "Behold my servant, whom I uphold, my chosen, in whom my soul delights; I have put my Spirit upon him; he will bring forth justice to the nations."[147] We know that Jesus was never apart from the Spirit. He was one with the Spirit, as are we, because the Spirit dwells in all believers,[148] though some seem to forget that and fail to stay open to the Spirit's leading.

> **Healthy churches are led by humble pastors. Humble pastors have humble intelligence through the humility factor, which includes openness to learning, others, and the Holy Spirit.**

The Humility Factor in Action
Questions to Ask and What to Look For:

1. Is there evidence of being a lifelong learner?
2. Do they seek and value the input of other people?
3. Does the pastor take the time to listen to the leading of the Holy Spirit through prayer and consideration without pushing their own agenda?

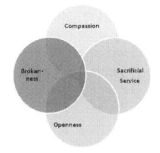

Brokenness

And they went to a place called Gethsemane. And he said to his disciples, "Sit here while I pray." And he took with him Peter and James and John, and began to be greatly distressed and troubled. And he said to them, "My soul is very sorrowful, even to death. Remain here and watch." And going a little farther, he fell on the ground and prayed that, if it were possible, the hour might pass from him. And he said, "Abba, Father, all things are possible for you. Remove this cup from me. Yet not what I will, but what you will."[149]

This is the account of Jesus in the Garden of Gethsemane on the night of His betrayal and arrest, leading to the mockery of a trial and crucifixion. Only days before, He had been given a king's welcome into the city, where He would spend His last days teaching crowds of people who wanted to hear the man they had heard could heal diseases, feed thousands, forgive sins, and hasten the kingdom of God on earth. However, on this night, His companions would abandon Him, His closest friend deny knowing Him, and the crowds turn against Him, and He would suffer the greatest travesty of justice the world has ever known. By every earthly definition, Jesus was a broken man, and He would soon allow His body to be broken and His blood to be poured out to save the people who rejected Him.

The next sign of the humility factor to look for in a potential pastor is brokenness. Of the seven signs of the humility factor, this may be the most difficult to define; however, it may be one of the easiest to recognize. When someone has been broken, it is evident, though unexplainable. One just knows, especially if they have been broken themselves. As I was writing this book and developing the concept of the humility factor, I had several people ask me specifically what I meant when I included brokenness in the attributes. The first thing I said was that humility comes from having failed. However, the more I wrestled with the meaning, I realized that there are many people who have failed, but remain arrogant, sometimes defiantly. Also, there are some people who are humble, but haven't necessarily had a significant failure in their lives. Brokenness can also be the result of losing the things of life which are meaningful to the person, such as relationships, loved ones, jobs, status, possessions, and reputation. Jesus had not failed, and He willingly gave up all He had, yet He allowed the breaking of His will in order to do the will of His Father. So, though I still believe experiencing failure and losing everything can contribute to brokenness, there is obviously still more to it. Let me continue to attempt to describe what I mean and why I include brokenness in the humility factor's seven signs.

Another time I see Jesus as being broken was when He spent 40 days in the desert being tempted by Satan at the beginning of His ministry. Due to the temptation to fulfill His own will and desires, especially for food and water, it is reasonable to believe that His will was broken as He submitted it to God. Then, when He emerged from the desert, His will was focused on God and His mission was clear.

Like Jesus, King David was a broken man, but because he had sinned against God by first falling into temptation with Bathsheba, then making matters progressively worse as he tried to fix the wrong he had done. He ultimately set in motion a cascade of sinful behavior including coercion, deceit, and murder, which cost him and all involved dearly. It is no surprise that the words of David are quite different and contrite in the latter days of his life in comparison to when he was young, confident, fearless, and invincible.

Unlike Jesus, David failed big time, but both were broken men, and both were restored to places of honor. Jesus, because of His obedience to the Father's will, was exalted: "So that at the name of Jesus every knee should bow, in heaven and on earth and under the earth, and every tongue confess that Jesus Christ is Lord, to the glory of God the Father."[150] David became known as "a man after God's heart," and some scholars believe that part of why David became remembered as such an esteemed leader was that through his brokenness, he was able to admit his error, correct his behavior, and fall before God, who restored the broken relationship.[151] Both broken, both honored, but for very different reasons and in entirely different circumstances.

Another attempt to describe brokenness comes from the practice of the breaking of a horse. This isn't directly from scripture, though there is a reference to it in the book of James: "If we put bits into the mouths of horses so that they obey us, we guide their whole bodies as well."[152] Anyone who has trained a horse knows that there is a point when the horse's will will break. It doesn't diminish the power of the horse, nor its majesty, strength, ability, beauty, or even confidence, but the horse comes to the point of submission to a higher power.

The common denominator in the horse, King David and Jesus is submission. Jesus, though Himself God, submitted to the Father and gave His life so that mankind could be restored. David, after destroying everything that he cared about, repented and submitted to God's authority once again. The horse, without losing any of its grand qualities, submits to its trainer and both benefit. Pastor J. Gordon Chamberlin discusses how "just as God could only use a suffering, humiliated, sacrificed man, so in humility and sacrifice can he use His church."[153] Pastor Douglas Hall speaks of the need for the church to engage in earnest repentance for its self-sufficiency,[154] and Bonem and Patterson teach that "building influence requires putting the prestige of your position aside"[155] and that an attitude of submission is not a loss of authority, but rather "the recognition of the source of authority."[156] Jesus, King David, and the horse all submitted to a higher authority.

I believe the best way to define brokenness in the humility factor is that the person has come to a submission point in their life and leadership position. They have an underlying broken will that no longer seeks its own way, but submits to a higher power. Because of it, God uses them, honors them, and blesses them. For pastors, this means that even with the authority they hold, they choose to submit to both the higher authority of God and the authority of the governing board of the church whose responsibility it is to hold the pastor accountable. If a pastor is unwilling to submit to either of these authorities, you will have trouble, which will keep the church from being healthy. Pastors need not worry about their position of leadership or their ability to do their job because, just as with the horse, submitting to the appropriate authorities does not take anything away from one's majesty, strength, ability, beauty, or even confidence. Though broken, the horse knows they are still all of those things, King David knew he was still king, and Jesus knew He was still God, just as the pastor knows that he is still the pastor and charged to lead the church.

In the immortal words of C. S. Lewis, full submission by a pastor to God will cause one to "be humble – delightfully humble, feeling the infinite relief of having for once, gotten rid of all the silly nonsense about your own dignity which has made you restless and unhappy all your life."[157] In a less profound but equally true analogy of being broken before God, Jim Collins calls this the ability of a leader to "be humble enough to aspire to be the dumbest person on the team."[158] Now that is humble and broken!

Christians are called to present themselves as a "living sacrifice,"[159] which King David wrote about soon after his adulterous affair with Bathsheba: "The sacrifices of God are a broken spirit. A broken and contrite heart, O God, you will not despise."[160] Brokenness is our sacrifice of submission, a quality which must be evident in our pastors. When it is, the humility which results from it will open the door for each of the other signs of the humility factor. Compassion will be unleashed, sacrificial service will be a natural outpouring, pastors will be open to others and to the Holy Spirit, and, as we will discuss in the rest of this chapter, self-awareness will increase and forgiveness and gratitude will become a way of life.

Healthy churches are led by humble pastors. Humble pastors have humble intelligence through the humility factor, which includes brokenness through submission to a higher authority.

The Humility Factor in Action
Questions to Ask and What to Look For:

1. Does the pastor insist on getting his way?
2. Is there evidence that they will submit to the higher authority of God and the governing board?
3. Though strong in abilities, is there a gentle and meek underlying spirit present?

Self-Awareness

The fifth sign of the humility factor is the attribute of self-awareness, which is a foundational trait in many of the positive leadership styles which will be discussed in the next chapter. Pastor Standish states it plainly, "Humble leaders are self-aware leaders,"[161] and McArthur-Blair states it as "knowing what we stand for when we become unhinged."[162]

Self-awareness is critical because, without an honest and intentional exploration of what really makes one tick, both an individual and their church can remain stuck in an unintentional state of bias and self-delusion. Pastors may sincerely believe that they care for the people in their congregation and in their community; however, when their actions are incongruent with their words, it becomes obvious that they are only kidding themselves. They must look within themselves and face the reality of their actual deeds to discover their true assumptions, beliefs, values, and biases.[163]

At its essence, self-awareness means that a pastor knows who they are in the sight of God, in the sight of man, and in the sight of self. If you look back at the pastors whom Pastor Standish highlighted as being humble, you will see a pattern of attitudes and behavior that demonstrate this principle. Those pastors know who they are and do not try to be someone they are not.

Self-Aware In the Sight of God

You will recall from the first chapter that it is important for all of us to remember that in comparison to God, we are not "all that," and that He trumps us every time. I once heard someone say that if we believe we're as powerful as God, "Try making an ant!" There is simply no possible way that we will ever be in God's league, so the sooner we get off our prideful high horse, the sooner we can all get back to doing the work which God has asked us to do. Pastors must have the self-awareness to know that they are not God, or anything close to Him. In the book *Exploring Christian Ethics*, Fedler states, "Leaders should be humble and grateful because they know 'human beings are not self-created.'"[164] Management legend Ken Blanchard is quoted as saying, "When we start to get a distorted image of our own importance and see ourselves as the center of the universe, we lose touch with who we really are as children of God."[165]

Part of being God's children, of course, provides for our inheritance in the kingdom that awaits us in heaven, described by the apostle Peter as "imperishable, undefiled, and unfading."[166] Knowing this gives us confidence, hope, and an understanding of our value in the sight of God; however, it should never become a source of pride. It is purely a gift of God, and not at all because of our own doing. Unfortunately, some lead pastors make the mistake of thinking that they are somehow, because of the position they hold, in a place next to God, or at least a notch or two higher than the people they were called to serve. Jesus deals with this directly when He states, "If anyone would be first, he must be last of all and servant of all"[167] and "Whoever would be great among you must be your servant, and whoever would be first among you must be slave of all. For even the Son of Man came not to be served but to serve, and to give his life as a ransom for many."[168]

Jesus didn't merely make these statements for others to abide by. He lived them and demonstrated that He was fully self-aware of Who He was in the sight of God. In Philippians, we see that Jesus, while knowing that He was "in the form of God, did not count equality with God a thing to be grasped"[169] and took on the form of a servant, humbling Himself in obedience for the glory of God. When He was arrested, He reminded his followers that He had the power to call down legions of angels,[170] but chose not to, and on the cross He continued to speak directly to His Heavenly Father and offered forgiveness and the promise of paradise to one of the robbers crucified next to Him. Jesus never forgot Who He was in the sight of God, nor should pastors.

Another reminder from scripture that is important for lead pastors to understand is that in the body of Christ, no one is to "think of himself more highly than he ought to think,"[171] but should "count others more significant than yourselves."[172] In 1 Corinthians 12, Paul goes into detail about the importance of each and every member of the body, emphasizing that one cannot dictate to another, nor declare that they are more important than another. "The eye cannot say to the hand, 'I have no need of you' nor again the head to the feet, 'I have no need of you.'" God has arranged the body with many parts, but it is still one body. God wants "no division in the body but that the member may have the same care for one another. If one suffers, all suffer together; if one member is honored, all rejoice together."[173] Far more can be said about this topic of equality in the body of Christ, but for now, pastors must be self-aware about who they are in the sight of God: unequal to God, but equal to, though not above, other people.

Self-Aware in the Sight of Man
The above discussion about a pastor's place in the body of Christ goes right along with the self-awareness needed in the sight of man. Usually a pastor does not begin their ministry thinking they are to be elevated above the people they serve in the congregation and with whom they serve alongside on the staff; however, congregations contribute to a pastor's feelings of superiority because of the way they treat them. Innocently, congregation members affirm the pastor's communication skills, show gratitude for pastoral care, admire biblical knowledge, and generally give a place of honor to their "man of God." As will be discussed in some of the leadership styles in the next chapter, these behaviors by the congregation can lead to a false sense of entitlement and

an inflated ego on the part of some pastors, who start to act as if they truly are above all others. I am not saying that appropriate affirmation should not be given, in fact, it is something which church people, especially church lay leaders, have a responsibility to do in order to support their pastor. However, it must be done in a manner that doesn't encourage the worst part of a person's ego to overtake the good work they are employed to do. So, with the help of the people they serve, it is important for pastors to have an authentic self-awareness of who they are in the sight of man.

There is an old adage that one "must not believe their own press," meaning that whether what others are saying about you is good, bad, true or fiction, it is most likely not fully true nor false. What we know of ourselves must come from God and within ourselves, not from what others, who may have an agenda and strings attached, may say about us. When we start to believe the bad things that are said, we lose confidence, doubt ourselves, and may change behaviors which we should continue. When we start to believe and accept the all the compliments, admiration, and praise as unequivocal truth, we're just asking for our pride to lead us to a great fall.[174]

Keeping a proper perspective of who we truly are in comparison to who others say we are is an important competency for self-aware leaders.[175] A good example is C. S. Lewis, who, in comparison to what others said of him in praise, states this about himself, "I am a very ordinary layman of the Church of England, not especially high nor especially low nor especially anything else."[176] In the book *Spiritual Leadership*, J. Oswald Sanders tells the story of a person of interest in the Salvation Army that further illustrates this point.

How Great Thou Art – How Great I'm Not

> On one occasion when Samuel Brengle was introduced as "the great Doctor Brengle," he noted in his diary:

If I appear great in their eyes, the Lord is most graciously helping me to see how absolutely nothing I am without Him, and helping me to keep little in my own eyes. He does use me. But I am so concerned that He uses me and that it is not of me the work is done. The axe cannot boast of the trees it has cut down. It could do nothing but for the woodsman. He made it, he sharpened it, and he used it. The moment he throws it aside, it becomes only old iron. O that I may never lose sight of this.[177]

Self-Aware in the Sight of Self

If one is honest, it's not that hard to stay humble when comparing oneself to God, and if they are vigilant, it's doable to stay humble when others around you are telling you how great you are. However, staying self-aware in the sight of self is the hardest of the three, because often the last thing we really want to do is to look inward, especially if we might see something that we don't like about ourselves. In his column in The Crosswalk website, Joe McKeever writes, "I've noticed a quirk of mine which I'm willing to bet is a widespread human frailty: When we look into the mirror, we do not see truth, but we see what we want to see."[178] True. We all know the story of the evil queen who relentlessly stared at a mirror and asked, "Who is the fairest of them all?" to which the magic mirror would reply that she was by far the fairest, until one day the mirror told the truth – that there was someone else in the kingdom who was actually the fairest. The story did not turn out well for the mirror, for after hearing the truth, the evil queen shattered it on the floor because she could not bear to hear or see the truth.

Man of La Mancha

In the immortal classic 1955 American musical, *Man of La Mancha* by Dale Wasserman, there is a tragic scene of self-discovery and awareness. Throughout the story, the main character, Don Quixote, has "sallied forth to right all wrongs" and, in the process, given everyone a tremendously powerful lesson in unconditional love. Unfortunately for him, his quest has all been part of a grand delusion brought about by old age and years of brooding over the perils and insensibilities of mankind. His family has gathered to help him snap out of his delusional state and live life once again in reality, though it be futile and devoid of hope and purpose. The family doctor performs a primitive form of intervention referred to as the "knight of the mirrors," and our hero is forced to look into the mirror and "see life as it truly is," resulting in his return to his aged and depressing real life. This procedure of forced self-awareness is successful; however, it begs the question as to if it might not have been kinder to allow an old man the dignity to live his last days in delusion.

▲ ▲ ▲

As Don Quixote discovered, looking into our personal mirror of self-awareness is hard, and it will often force us to deal with things we don't care to. By looking into the mirror, we see the things about our hurts, habits, and hang-ups which we need to change, but it also can be incredibly valuable in our quest to become the person God created us to be as we begin to make adjustments that will move us toward what Anjana Sen calls the "center of humility,"[179] where one must remain as alert as a tightrope walker as they become self-aware. It takes courage to face our fears and failures to deal with the parts of ourselves that aren't what God wants, such as pride. However, when we look into the mirror we also see the signs of God's amazing creativity and His touch on our lives, because being self-aware is not only about the things on which we need to work, but also the things in which we are awesome. Awesome, because God made us that way.

Self-aware pastors have a great understanding of what they lack, but also in what they excel, and by keeping their sight of self under the umbrella of their sight of God, it will be a powerfully positive tool for being an effective leader who possesses humble intelligence. By knowing who they truly are, they are free to do what they were created to do and free to not do that for which they weren't created. Self-aware leaders know that "leadership is not about position, title, or the role we want to play. For those who claim to love and follow Jesus, leading in His Kingdom involves service, subordination, and even slavery."[180]

> **Healthy churches are led by humble pastors. Humble pastors have humble intelligence through the humility factor, which includes self-awareness of who they are in the sight of God, man, and self.**

The Humility Factor in Action
Questions to Ask and What to Look For:

1. Does the pastor understand where he stands in comparison to God?
2. Does the pastor revel in the adulation of their congregation?
3. Does the pastor have an authentic view of his strengths and weaknesses?
4. Is the pastor honest with himself?

THE HUMILITY FACTOR

Forgiveness

While the attribute of brokenness was the hardest sign to describe but easily recognized, the next sign of the humility factor—forgiveness—is probably the easiest to define, but the most difficult to put into action. And, like brokenness, it is easy to spot if it is there, but even easier if it is not. All believers understand and accept the forgiveness we receive from God through the blood of Jesus. We embrace the words that assure us of the forgiveness of sins, such as, "We have the forgiveness of our trespasses according to the riches of His grace;"[181] "As far as the east is from the west, so far does he remove our transgressions from us;"[182] and Jesus' own words, "This is my blood of the covenant, which is poured out for many for the forgiveness of sins,"[183] and the almost unfathomable words spoken on the cross, "Father, forgive them."[184]

At the core of our faith is the forgiveness we gratefully receive, but that's when it gets hard. Accepting forgiveness from God is one thing, but then having to apply forgiveness in our own lives to others who have wronged us is much more difficult. One might think this wouldn't be that hard to do, considering what God did for us. Sarah Ban Breathnach, the author of *Simple Abundance*, states, "Forgiveness is a form of gratitude. When we forgive others, we show them the mercy that we have often received and been thankful for."[185] However, unfortunately, many of us can think of people about whom we feel morally justified in holding our grudge,[186] and of multiple times when good, God-fearing Christians have a disagreement that is never resolved, destroying a relationship and often poisoning the fellowship for years and sometimes generations to come.

On the flip side, it has been written that intentional forgiveness is "a way for individuals to repair damaged relationships... by forgiving others, negative emotions can be overcome and resentment is let go,"[187] which is why this is a critical part of the humility factor to look for in a pastor. I've heard it said by many pastors that if the devil wants to easily take down a church, it won't happen through large-scale programmatic failures, money problems, or even scandal, but through strained and broken relationships between the people. If he can divide God's people and get them fighting and holding on to bitterness toward each other, the church becomes unhealthy and irrelevant in the fight for eternity.

As you evaluate potential pastors, look for evidence that they not only can accept forgiveness, but can also willingly extend it to others. If they are unable to do that, they not only disqualify themselves as an example of what Christ has called pastors to model in the way of forgiveness, but place in jeopardy their own forgiveness from God. Jesus is recorded as teaching on this very issue in three of the four gospels.

- Matthew 16:14-15: "For if you forgive others their trespasses, your Heavenly Father will also forgive you, but if you do not forgive others their trespasses, neither will your Father forgive your trespasses."[188]
- Mark 11:25-26: "And whenever you stand praying, forgive, if you have anything against anyone, so that your Father also who is in heaven may forgive you your trespasses."[189]
- Luke 6:37: "Forgive, and you will be forgiven...for with the measure you use it will be measured back to you."[190]

▲ ▲ ▲

The Parable of the Wicked Servant

> Therefore the kingdom of heaven may be compared to a king who wished to settle accounts with his servants. When he began to settle, one was brought to him who owed him ten thousand talents. And since he could not pay, his master ordered him to be sold, with his wife and children and all that he had, and payment to be made. So the servant fell on his knees, imploring him, "Have patience with me, and I will pay you everything." And out of pity for him, the master of that servant released him and forgave him the debt. But when the same servant went out, he found one of his fellow servants who owed him a hundred denarii, and seizing him, he began to choke him, saying, "Pay what you owe." So his fellow servant fell down and pleaded with him, "Have patience with me, and I will pay you." He refused and went and put him in prison until he should pay the debt. When his fellow servants saw what had taken place, they were greatly distressed, and they went and reported to their master all that had taken place. Then his master summoned him and said to him, "You wicked servant! I forgave you all that debt because you pleaded with me. And should not you have had mercy on your fellow servant, as I had mercy on you?" And in anger his master delivered him to the jailers, until he should pay all his debt. So also my Heavenly Father will do to every one of you, if you do not forgive your brother from your heart.[191]

⸺ ⸺ ⸺

If Jesus devoted this much teaching to the topic of forgiveness, and said that one's own forgiveness will be withheld if they do not forgive others, it must be critically important. This is why forgiveness is included in the humility factor. Here is an example of forgiveness by a pastor told by Ken Sande, the founder of Peacemaker Ministries. As you read it, imagine how refreshing it would be if our church leaders acted in this way, and what a tremendous impact it would have on those who are not yet in the fold.

Breaking News: Pastor and Elder Forgive Each Other and Seek Unity and Peace

> The pastor of a church I attended during college clearly understood the importance of seeking peace with an estranged brother. He demonstrated this the Sunday I brought a friend named Cindy to church for the first time. I had met Cindy at school and learned that she was struggling in her spiritual life, largely because the church she attended provided little biblical teaching. Thinking that she might find meaningful instruction and encouragement from my church, I had invited her to worship with me one Sunday. I was unprepared for what took place shortly after Cindy and I took our seats, because I had forgotten that during the previous week's Sunday school period my pastor and an elder had gotten into a public argument. Pastor Woods called for the attention of the congregation and asked the elder with whom he had quarreled to join him at the pulpit. "As most of you know," Pastor Woods said, "Kent and I had an argument during Sunday school last week. Our emotions got out of hand, and we said some things that should have been discussed in private."
>
> As I thought of the first impression Cindy must be getting, my stomach sank. "Of all the days to bring someone to

church," I thought, "why did I pick this one?" I was sure this incident would discourage Cindy from coming to my church again. Pastor Woods put his arm around Kent's shoulders and went on. "We want you to know that we met that same afternoon to resolve our differences. By God's grace, we came to understand each other better, and we were fully reconciled. But we need to tell you how sorry we are for disrupting the unity of this fellowship, and we ask for your forgiveness for the poor testimony we gave last week."

Many eyes were filled with tears as Pastor Woods and Kent prayed together. Unfortunately, I was so worried about what Cindy might be thinking that I completely missed the significance of what had happened. Making a nervous comment to Cindy, I opened the hymnal to our first song and hoped she would forget about the whole incident. The rest of the service was a blur, and before long I was driving her home. I made light conversation for a few minutes, but eventually Cindy referred to what had happened: "I still can't believe what your pastor did this morning. I've never met a minister in my church who had the courage and humility to do what he did. I'd like to come to your church again."

During subsequent visits, Cindy's respect for my pastor and for Kent continued to grow, and before long she made our church her spiritual home. She saw real evidence of God's presence and power in those two men. Their humility highlighted God's strength and helped Cindy to take Christ more seriously. As a result, she committed herself to Christ and began to grow in her faith. As I watch that growth continue to this day, I still thank God for those two men and their willingness to obey the Lord's call to peace and unity.[192]

▲ ▲ ▲

> *Healthy churches are led by humble pastors. Humble pastors have humble intelligence through the humility factor, which includes the ability to extend forgiveness to others.*

The Humility Factor in Action
Questions to Ask and What to Look For:

1. Does the pastor harbor bitterness toward any person, group, or their previous church?
2. Has the pastor passed along the same level of forgiveness which was given to them?
3. Do they reconcile broken relationships when they occur?

▲ ▲ ▲

Gratitude

According to the dictionary, grateful and thankful are synonyms, each meaning the other when defined,[193] so, as we introduce the last of the seven signs of the humility factor, note that the Bible has well over 1000 references to gratitude, thanksgiving, and all forms of each word within the scriptures, including multiple accounts of Jesus giving thanks to His Heavenly Father in a variety of setting and circumstances, most notably prior to breaking the bread that symbolically represented His own broken body at the last supper on the night before He was crucified. Even when pointing directly to the horror of the cross, Jesus remained thankful for what He had been given.

According to Ron Edmondson, "Humble leaders recognize that all good gifts come from above,"[194] for which they must remain thankful. Scripture simply states, "Give thanks to the Lord, for He is good,"[195] pointing directly to the fact that God Himself isn't only the source of good things, but "good" itself. When writing about servant leaders, Dirk van Dierendonek and Kathleen Patterson state,

> Gratitude can be defined as a feeling of thankful appreciation for the good things received in life. We assume that grateful leaders have a sense of abundance, will appreciate the simple pleasures in life, are appreciative of the contribution of others, and will acknowledge the importance of expressing gratitude toward those in their environment.[196]

Pastors who possess humble intelligence are grateful people. They recognize the good things which God has put in their lives, which translates into an appreciation for the others around them with whom they work and serve. When something good happens, they give the credit to God and they outwardly model thankfulness to the people they lead. When circumstances aren't ideal, or in times when the challenges of life are mounting, a grateful pastor will remain optimistic and trust in God's provision as is written, "Give thanks in all circumstances; for this is the will of God in Christ Jesus for you."[197] At no point will a pastor who has the humility factor's attribute of gratitude feel or act entitled to special treatment or bitter when they don't get the things they may want. They don't see their position as deserving of special treatment or "places of honor."[198] Instead, they follow scripture's command, "And whatever you do, in word or deed, do everything in the name of the Lord Jesus, giving thanks to God the Father through him."[199] For whatever the circumstances, the reward, or the compensation, a pastor with humble intelligence is grateful.

▲ ▲ ▲

Through Grace to Grace

    A friend and former colleague of mine is an outstanding example of a humble pastor who has consistently modeled gratitude to everyone around him. Paul Gilbert is the pastor of Grace Fellowship Church in Buffalo, Wyoming. The town is small, less than 5000 people, and the church, though one of the largest in the town, is a reflection of its surroundings. Paul has been the pastor for several years, and the church has grown and added worship services due to the good work being done. Paul is a gentle, caring man with strong communication skills, a great sense of humor, excellent administrative skills and the know-how to get things done. Before he went to Grace Church, he and I worked on many large projects together and had a blast.

    Paul's journey to humble intelligence was not one which he would have chosen, though. He began his ministry as a highly effective pastor of growing churches, which led him to denomination-wide leadership positions; he was on the fast track for bigger and greater things. However, his life took some major detours, which he would tell you caused him to lose virtually everything, including relationships, job, influence, and possessions. He lost his position, and by the time I met him, he was a broken and humbled man who was working hard to rebuild his life and ministry.

Through a long chain of circumstances, God opened the door for Paul to become the lead pastor at Grace Church, which has been a very positive step back toward the life he was created to live, but now with a full grasp of humble intelligence, because he now lives every attribute of the humility factor.

One of the things that impresses me so about Paul is that he has always appeared grateful for whatever blessings, provisions, and circumstances God had given him. I don't recall Paul ever complaining that he should have more in position, prestige, or material possession, even though I knew that he was getting by on far less than he had had in the past. His spirit was always one of optimism and faith and he often helped me through times when I needed to keep my own chin up and look to God for encouragement. I believe that because Paul had gone through the dark times, he was able to be absolutely grateful for every good thing. He is the living example of giving thanks to God with his "whole heart and recounting all of God's wonderful deeds."[200]

▲ ▲ ▲

Grace Church has greatly benefited from having Paul as their pastor. The last time I spoke with him, the church attendance had nearly doubled and they had added a Saturday night service to their weekend schedule. The church is on an upswing and having more and more of a positive impact in their community. I believe that much of the reason is because they have a humble pastor who has the experience to help them to be successful and effective, and has attained humble intelligence, which helps them to be healthy.

Healthy churches are led by humble pastors. Humble pastors have humble intelligence through the humility factor, which includes being grateful in all circumstances.

The Humility Factor in Action
Questions to Ask and What to Look For:

1. Does the pastor show gratitude for what is provided by God and the church?
2. Does the pastor appear to feel entitled to material rewards and the places of honor?
3. When circumstances are tough, does the pastor still acknowledge the blessings of God?

There you have it. **The humility factor consists of seven attributes of humility modeled by Jesus Christ in words and actions. When all are present and collectively applied to a leader's life, these create humble intelligence. When humble intelligence is applied to any leadership style, it improves it because the leader leads more like Jesus led.**

That's the humility factor and humble intelligence! In the next chapter, we will take a deep dive into the leadership styles which can be found in pastors in churches, then apply the collective humility factor to them and see how they are transformed and improved. Take a breath! The next chapter covers a lot of information.

CHAPTER 4

So Many Pastoral Leaders to Choose From!

Pastoral Leadership Styles

Ralph Waldo Emerson states, "It is one of the most beautiful compensations of life that no man can sincerely try to help another without helping himself."[201] This is a good description of the positive side of pastoral ministry. While there are certainly challenges that confront the person who has committed their life to serving Jesus through the local church, there are also tremendous rewards that come from putting one's own needs aside in favor of others. One of the things that happens is that the more one places their focus on blessing others, the more they will, in turn, be blessed themselves. God just works it out that way and it's a great perk of ministry. Referring to all forms of work, theologian Ben Witherington III states that work "is not a secular activity; it is a sacred one originally ordained by God, and so it must be undertaken in a holy way."[202] Therefore since the work a pastor performs takes the holiness of work even further, it raises the bar as to the qualifications and standards individuals must meet in order to be considered for a pastoral position. Church lay leaders know this and feel the pressure to find the perfect person for the job. They typically look for someone who meets the criteria of what is often referred to as the "great man" leadership theory, even if they don't know it at the time.

This theory originated in the 19th century and views great leaders as virtual heroes – highly influential individuals who, due to their personal charisma, intelligence, wisdom, or political skill, use their power in a way that has a decisive impact. Although it's been around for a long time, it is still a standard by which many organizations, especially churches, operate when choosing their next leader. Characteristics of a "great man" include focus, confidence, integrity, transparency, innovation, passion, patience and authenticity. They are also relational, decisive, empowering, positive, generous, persistent, insightful and more![203] Who wouldn't want a pastor with all of these qualities wrapped up in one package? In describing a great lead pastor, Bonem and Patterson state,

> Those with a leader's temperament have a strong desire for the ministry to reach its fullest potential, and they always work toward that goal. "Let someone else worry about it" is not in their vocabulary. They dream big dreams about the things that God is going to do in the larger organization, and they stand ready to do their part when God creates the opportunity.[204]

Again, what church board member wouldn't want to find and hire this person? Not only would the new lead pastor be considered a heroic leader,[205] but so, too, would the board members who hired them. Let's face it, gender aside, when churches are looking to hire their next pastor, they want a great man. Unfortunately, sometimes with the great man come great issues of ego, a lack of servanthood, selfish ambition, a command-and-control style, and more dark qualities that we will explore later in this chapter. However, also with this type of leader come vision, transformation, courage, optimism and many other positive qualities, which we will also discuss in a moment.

One other issue that can also come with picking a "great man" is the perception held by people in the congregation, who may exhibit an exaggerated level of awe of the person simply because of the position they hold, which can lead to an inflated sense of self-importance by the pastor. All too often pastors are considered God's anointed messengers by the congregation, and thus infallible. This isn't because of the person themselves, but rather because of their position. Somehow a person is a mere mortal at one moment, then, once they accept the job, they are elevated above everyone else. Problems arise because too often the pastor begins to believe that they are indeed superior and special. Standish discusses this when he says,

> We are distinct and special not because of any qualities or abilities we ourselves possess. Our unique qualities are gifts from God that come from God's Spirit breathed into us…nothing we do by our own power….Sin emerges as we cultivate the belief that our uniqueness is due to our own efforts independent of God….Humility begins the process of restoring us to an appreciation of God's gift of Spirit and life, whose effect is to enable us to grow in Spirit.[206]

Note that we can acknowledge that God has created each of us as unique and special, but He is the one who must be given the credit. People's perception that someone is superior simply because of position is merely that, perception, and it does not make it true. The following story, which I borrow from Simon Sinek's book *Leaders Eat Last*, further illustrates how position can wrongly alter how people view and value an individual. This time it isn't a story of a pastor, but rather a former U.S. Under Secretary of Defense.

DR. JOHN PLASTOW

The Ceramic Cup

While making a speech at a large conference, he took his place on the stage and began talking, sharing his prepared remarks with the audience. He paused to take a sip of coffee from the Styrofoam cup he'd brought on stage with him. He took another sip, looked down at the cup and smiled. "You know," he said, interrupting his own speech, "I spoke here last year. I presented at this same conference on this same stage. But last year, I was still the Under Secretary," he said. "I flew here in business class and when I landed, there was someone waiting for me at the airport to take me to my hotel. Upon arriving at my hotel," he continued, "there was someone else waiting for me. They had already checked me into the hotel, so they handed me my key and escorted me up to my room. The next morning, when I came down, again there was someone waiting for me in the lobby to drive me to this same venue that we are in today. I was taken through a back entrance, shown to the greenroom and handed a cup of coffee in a beautiful ceramic cup."

But this year, as I stand here to speak to you, I am no longer the Under Secretary. I flew here coach class and when I arrived at the airport yesterday, there was no one there to meet me. I took a taxi to the hotel, and when I got there, I checked myself in and went by myself to my room. This morning, I came down to the lobby and caught another taxi to come here. I came in the front door and found my way backstage. Once there, I asked one of the techs if there was any coffee. He pointed to a coffee machine on a table against the wall. So, I walked over and poured myself a cup of coffee into this here Styrofoam cup.

It occurs to me, the ceramic cup they gave me last year was never meant for me at all. It was meant for the position I held. I deserve a Styrofoam cup. This is the most important lesson I can impart to all of you. All of the perks, all the benefits and advantages you may get for the rank or position you hold, they aren't meant for you. They are meant for the role you fill. And when you leave your role, which eventually you will, they will give the ceramic cup to the person who replaces you. Because you only ever deserve a Styrofoam cup."[207]

▲ ▲ ▲

This story is a good reminder that position is not the person, and serves as good advice to pastors to not start thinking more of themselves than they deserve. Congregation members may consider the role of the pastor as a sacred one, however, they should never forget that the person filling that role is as human as the next. As a bonus, this story also provides a comparison of the ceramic cup in the story to our position as mere humble jars of clay – fragile, easily broken, and moldable by the master potter. We must remember that the true power to lead belongs to God and not to us regardless of the position we fill.[208]

Help Wanted: The Job Description of a Pastor

A quick Google search produces a wide variety of "job descriptions for pastors." They range from the standard teach-and-preach models of many denominationally-affiliated churches to the lead-and-feed model of non-denominational evangelical congregations. All reflect the values, style, preferences, doctrine, habits, and even hang-ups of a particular church or denomination, and the job descriptions paint the far-reaching and ambitious hopes, dreams, and expectations a congregation has for their next lead pastor, for a modest salary, of course! Some of the descriptions are heady, while others focus on being relational. Some are super spiritual and based on the biblical mandates of what qualifies one to be a pastor, while others are light and friendly. There are even some that are comical, and some which cause one to wonder if they are serious.

One of the things that quickly becomes evident when viewing the many posted pastoral job descriptions is that neither the position of pastor nor the description of their duties is static.[209] As expected, one of the first qualifications people look for is a lead pastor's ability to preach, and to do so from an advanced and educated point of reference. However, problems arise in some congregations that expect the pastor to be the expert, but not to come off as if they know more than the people to whom they preach. Kinnison states, "I know of no other profession in the world where a person can be as highly trained as a pastoral leader and be maligned by her or his clients for being so well trained."[210] It's quite a paradox, as pastoral candidates are expected to have an advanced degree to be worthy of hire, but then viewed as a threat if they know too much!

To sidestep for a moment, one thought to consider about preaching being the primary requirement is whether the lead pastor must be a preacher at all. In some cases, the best leader may be a person who has training and skills in an entirely different area of ministry. I agree that preaching is crucial to the church, but I have long believed that church lay leaders might want to consider this to be the responsibility of a teaching pastor position, or a team of teachers, allowing the lead pastor to operate fully from their strengths in transformation, administration, vision, shepherding, worship, etc. It's not the standard model, but it is worth considering, especially in this age when the newest generation of church attenders (Millennials) express their desire to be led by example, service, and mentoring, rather than being preached at,[211] but that is a topic for another day. Still, there are many churches that have adopted a team approach to preaching and teaching. Instead of one preacher, congregations are given the benefit of multiple voices and points of view that work together to bring the message each week. Relating to the topic of a lead pastor not having to be the preacher, there are churches that are also beginning to adopt a team approach to the lead or senior pastor role. Instead of one lead, they may have two or more.

Four Senior Pastors?

> An example of this team model is Bayside Church in Granite Bay, CA, which has recently installed four of their pastors to serve together as the senior pastors. Granted, three out of the four would be considered primary teacher/preachers, but the fourth is the worship pastor, who, while he does occasionally deliver the message, mostly serves in the worship role, supporting my belief that the best leaders don't necessarily come out of the traditional view that lead pastors must preach and that the preachers must be the lead pastor. It will be interesting to see how this works and if other churches are courageous enough to try this non-traditional approach. We should all stay tuned.

⋏ ⋏ ⋏

The idea that preaching may not need to be in the toolbox of your next lead pastor is certainly a current road less taken by most churches, so let's get back to what is typically in the job description, which begins with preaching and then includes many other duties. Author Brian Croft stated,

The modern pastor is expected to be a preacher, counselor, administrator, PR guru, fund-raiser, and hand-holder. Depending upon the size of the church he serves, he may have to be an expert on youth...something of an accountant, janitor, evangelist, small groups expert, and excellent chair of committees, a team player and a transparent leader.[212]

Kinnison describes congregations as expecting the pastor to accomplish the entire description above and more as "the vendor of religious goods and services," but in reality only Jesus Himself could fulfill this, assuming he was able to get an interview, since he doesn't have much experience in a local church and has no video resume of his preaching style posted online. Some might even suggest he was a drifter and can't be trusted to show up for work!

The following is a random selection of denominational descriptions floating around the web. It includes the oversight and leading of the sacraments of communion, baptism, and weddings, in addition to confirmations, funerals, worship collaboration, staff meetings, biblical interpretation, reporting to denominational hierarchy, vision casting, a host of social activities, and more. All of this is for an average annual median salary of $55,287.[213]

Church blogger and consultant Ron Edmondson lists the "16 unknown roles of a pastor" as counselor, career coach, business advisor, custodian, arbitrator, social worker, volunteer coordinator, events manager, CEO, fundraiser, recruiter, trainer, scholar, writer, manager, and public relations manager, plus a bonus role of politician.[214] There are also, of course, the biblical qualifications listed in the New Testament books of 1 Timothy, Titus, and 1 Peter that outline what it means for a pastor to live above reproach. All together there are 17 qualifications on this list: being devoted to one wife, a good manager of his family, a faithful steward, humble and not arrogant, gentle and not quick-tempered, sober and not a drunkard, peaceful, not greedy, hospitable, lover of good, self-controlled, upright in relationships, holy, able to teach, spiritually mature, respectable, and a good example to the flock.[215]

Survey Data Results and Discovery

In preparation for this book, two surveys were conducted that contribute to our discussion of the desirable qualities and characteristics that lead pastors should possess. Using a boosted post, I used Facebook to ask congregation members one simple question: "What are the three to five most important leadership characteristics a lead/senior pastor should have?" I deliberately kept it simple so as not to lead the respondents in any way, as I truly wanted to discover what they were thinking without any prompting from me.

The second survey was a little more directed and was a targeted mailing to lead pastors. I asked several questions:

1. How long have you been in vocational ministry?
2. What are the three to five most important leadership characteristics a lead/senior pastor should have?"
3. What is and what is not working in church leadership today?
4. Describe the biggest challenges you face in your relationship with your board.
5. To whom are you accountable?

In both surveys, I appealed to their desire to make a positive difference in the Kingdom of God, and I offered a chance to win an Amazon gift card. Pastors are listed in the book! The response for each was an approximate 4% sampling of those invited to participate.

Congregation Member Survey

The results of the congregation member survey were interesting and confirming, but not necessarily surprising. As I assessed the responses from the survey, I was able to reference the humility factor signs and see if random congregation members were thinking as I thought they might be. Of the seven humility factor signs, compassion was ranked #1 by a wide margin over all others. In fact, 57.9% included it. This was unprompted, so slightly unexpected, though it goes along with the current cultural desires of the Millennial generation, which greatly values and seeks meaningful relationships in their church experience. Humility and compassion tied for the #1 individual response overall, which is both surprising and not, because humility is typically not a trait for which church boards state they are looking during the hiring process, but one to which people are generally drawn in a leader, even if it is unstated.

While not part of the humility factor signs, topics relating to integrity, honesty, and character were listed by 49.1% of participants. "Integrity" and "honesty" were both also in the top five of the individual traits identified, and also the #1 trait identified in the pastoral edition of the survey. This emphasis on integrity and character is not at all surprising because in organizations, cross-cultural groups, and virtually every country across the globe, the number one trait people look for in a leader is whether they can be trusted. People everywhere want honest leaders.

Also in the congregational survey, all seven of the humility factor signs show up in the responses in some manner:

- Compassion   57.9%
- Service   26.3%
- Openness   26.3%
- Brokenness   17.5%
- Self-Awareness   14.0%

- Forgiveness 3.5%
- Gratitude 3.5%

It is interesting and perhaps disturbing that forgiveness and gratitude barely show up on the list of desired pastoral traits, each at only 3.5%, especially with the emphasis scripture places on both. This is indeed a sign that work needs to be done in the leadership characteristics of our churches' pastors.

Of the non-humility factor signs in the individual responses in the survey, three categories emerged into which all of the other responses were grouped.

Personal attributes were identified by 78.9%, and included:

- Accountability
- Anointing
- Commitment to the Lord
- Devotion to God
- Discernment
- Draws people to Jesus, not himself
- Exemplary morals
- Faith
- God loving/fearing
- Godly example of life priorities
- Godly person
- Humility
- Joy in the Lord
- Know the Bible by living it 24/7
- Love of Christ
- Loyalty
- Passion for Jesus
- Patience

- Respectful
- Security in their identity in Christ
- Self-discipline
- Sense of humor
- Sincerity
- Spirit-led
- Strong prayer life

Leadership skills were identified by 77.1%, and included:

- Ability to actively lead
- Ability to delegate
- Ability to get staff to work as a team
- Ability to inspire
- Ability to make hard decisions
- Adept at empowerment/delegating
- Business sense
- Competence
- Fearless even when opposed
- Gives team members latitude to make decisions
- Initiative
- Intelligence
- Knowing your parishioners
- Motivation
- Not pushy
- Organization
- Personality
- Relatable
- Stays current with modern culture
- Strict safeguards
- Time management
- Vision
- Wisdom

Pastoral technical skills were identified by 58.6% and included:

- Ability to teach the Bible well
- Able to present sermon without reading it
- Avid reader
- Bible based
- Communication
- Effective preaching
- Engaging speaker
- Fidelity to Scripture
- Fully grounded in the Word of God
- Humility in theology
- Knowledge of the Bible
- Leadership skills to share Word of God
- Patience to teach and disciple followers
- Shepherd (selfless protector)
- Show Bible's relevance by bringing it to life
- Strong worship leader
- Teacher of God's Word

It is quite interesting that there are significantly fewer characteristics on the "pastoral technical skills" list than those in the "personal attributes" list, as often search committees have a tendency to gravitate to candidates with more technical skills than personal attributes, which is an example of the incongruence between what we say and what we do. We often say we want a shepherd, but we look for a CEO.

Pastoral Survey

The results of the pastoral survey were very surprising on one hand, as 51 different phrases were used, and much as expected on the other. As to the question of what traits they felt were important in a pastor, there was no consensus of terms. When categorized, the responses were similar to those of the congregational survey, but with a more "pastoral" tone. An example of this is that in place of the humility factor attribute of sacrificial service, one pastor states it as "spiritual paradigm for mission and ministry" and another responded "self-differentiation" instead of openness (self-awareness). Others identified communication skills, knowledge, decisiveness, and love for God, to name a few.

Not surprising at all was that 81 percent of the respondents had been in vocational ministry for over ten years, and the things which these pastors believe are not working in the church today range from tradition to trendiness, including institutional preservation, maintaining congregational happiness, lack of vision and mission, unrealistic expectations that lead to poor work-life balance, financial resources held hostage by outdated methods and preferences, and a focus on audience sovereignty over God's sovereignty. In many cases, the frustration has to do with the expectation that they be more of a CEO rather than a shepherd, a priority of numbers over spiritual growth, and the feeling that their lay leaders want the pastor to be the one to "do ministry" rather than its being a collaborative effort, with everyone getting their hands dirty while serving to meet the needs of the community. At the same time, there is a general positivity toward trends back to collaborative decision-making, a resurgence of accountability structure and a reliance on the Holy Spirit and prayer-discerned vision. All in all, the view from pastors is a mixed bag of frustration and optimism.

Challenges with lay leaders continue primarily due to power struggles, differences in Bible knowledge and interpretation, vision, priorities, and the need for innovation. The most interesting result of the pastoral survey is that most list God as the one to whom they are accountable. This is interesting not because it is ultimately true, but because it appears to be common that pastors are not generally open to or welcoming of the input of the lay leadership. It is most evident in some responses that accountability to the board is more of an annoyance and inconvenience than a blessing. There is also little mention of accountability to the general congregation, the group which they were hired to serve. The following true story is a good example of a pastor's view of accountability gone awry.

Royal Behavior

> "I hate being treated like an employee" was the grumbling of a pastor who had received some pushback from his board the previous evening. Something had happened and a decision had been made by the long-term pastor with which some of the board members disagreed. This was highly unusual because each of the eleven members of the board had been handpicked by the pastor and typically went along with anything they wanted to do, regardless of its merit or apparent complications. The pastor simply was allowed to do whatever he pleased, and he had done so for many years. The board and the church members who chose to remain believed that the pastor was the anointed one and treated his family and him much like the chief priests of Jesus' time were treated, with privilege, wealth, and the willingness to look the other way if a questionable decision or conspicuous consumption arose. The pastor and his family were the royalty of the church, and this particular pastor enjoyed every perk and privilege it provided. He was accustomed to being the supreme leader, and certainly not an employee.
>
> So, when some of his handpicked board members openly opposed him, the pastor shut down the meeting,

walked out of the room, and convened a haphazard staff meeting the next morning for the purpose of venting his anger and demanding that the staff show their unconditional loyalty and stand with him. Threatening the staff, he stated, "I am the man of God and my decisions will not be questioned!" The staff remained quiet for fear of termination, and because by this time, they were accustomed to their leader's rants and subsequent periods of melancholy and self-imposed isolation in which there would be a barrage of hurtful emails to anyone who was perceived as not sharing his outrage, even to the point of being punished by being removed from email groups and the ultimate, unfriending on Facebook. Most of the staff learned to ride out the storm and continue to do what they could for the good of the ministry. Unfortunately, though, even though each of these episodes would eventually blow over, it was a pattern that would always resurface the next time anyone questioned the pastor's viewpoint. Opposing thoughts, or even the mere asking of a question, was considered disloyal and taken very personally.

Within a few days, things settled down and the staff was able to get back to serving the people of the church and doing what they were hired to do, all the while trying to ignore the childishness of the senior pastor, at least until the next time.

⊥ ⊥ ⊥

Of course, not all pastors have this misguided self-view and hostility toward those who might question them. Some share good relationships with their lay leaders and are willing to listen to input from the congregation, lay leaders, and staff members. Unfortunately, though, there are some pastors, like the one in the above example, that need to apply the attributes of the humility factor.

On a Lighter Note

Before we turn our discussion to the various leadership styles and traits available to you, let's take a moment to smile and perhaps laugh out loud at some of the more comical pastoral job descriptions and expectations. One writer provides the following list of potential candidates for their church's senior pastor position and a tongue-in-cheek evaluation. On the surface, you would expect some of these celebrities from the Bible to be outstanding candidates for the job, but as you will read, they fall short of the standards set. Here are a few examples.

- **Adam**: Good man, but has problems with his wife.
- **Noah:** Prone to unrealistic building projects.
- **Abraham**: There is a report of an offer to share his wife with another man.
- **Joseph**: A big thinker, but a braggart, believes in dream-interpreting, and has a prison record.
- **Moses**: A poor communicator, and some say he left an earlier church over a murder charge.
- **David**: The most promising leader of all except for the affair he had with his neighbor's wife.
- **Elisha**: Reported to have lived with a single widow while at his former church.
- **Hosea**: A tender and loving pastor but our people could never handle his wife's occupation.
- **John:** Says he is a Baptist, but definitely doesn't dress like one.
- **Peter**: Too blue collar. Has a bad temper—has even been known to curse.

- **Paul**: Powerful CEO-type leader and fascinating preacher; however, short on tact, unforgiving with younger ministers, harsh and has been known to preach all night.
- **Timothy**: Too young.
- **Jesus**: Has had popular times, but once, when his church grew to 5000, he managed to offend them all and his church dwindled down to twelve people. Seldom stays in one place very long. And, of course, he's single.
- **Judas**: His references are solid. A steady plodder. Conservative. Good connections. Knows how to handle money. We're inviting him to preach this Sunday. Possibilities here.[216]

As you can see, not even Jesus was the perfect pastoral candidate for the above church, but here is a job description for the perfect pastor which you might find helpful from the website of Friar Tommy Lane.

- The perfect pastor preaches exactly 10 minutes.
- He condemns sin roundly, but never hurts anyone's feelings.
- He works from 8 am until midnight and is also the church janitor.
- The perfect pastor makes $40 a week, wears good clothes, drives a good car, buys good books, and donates $30 a week to the church.
- He is 29 years old and has 40 years experience.
- Above all, he is handsome.
- The perfect pastor has a burning desire to work with teenagers, and he spends most of his time with the senior citizens.
- He smiles all the time with a straight face because he has a sense of humor that keeps him seriously dedicated to his church.

- He makes 15 home visits a day and is always in his office to be handy when needed.
- The perfect pastor always has time for church council and all of its committees.
- He never misses the meeting of any church organization and is always busy evangelizing the unchurched.[217]

▲ ▲ ▲

Now that we have had a moment to chuckle at these ridiculous examples, let's turn our attention to the many different styles and traits you will observe in individuals who apply to be your next lead pastor. Keep in mind that all have good qualities and bad, and each can be effective in their own right, however, many have a dark side. However, they will all be immensely better leaders, and your church will enjoy the benefits of being healthier, when the humility factor is added to their styles and traits. Leaders come in all shapes, sizes, personalities, gifts, talents, and styles. So do pastors. On the buffet of pastors, there is a huge assortment of entrées from which to choose.

The Pastoral Leadership Buffet

The wonderful thing about a world-class buffet, whether it be at Caesar's Palace in Las Vegas (my personal favorite), on the Queen Mary in Long Beach, CA, or at The Plaza in New York City, is that there is not only something for every preferred taste, but every selection is awesome. There is simply not a poorly-prepared dish in the bunch. One going through the buffet line may not personally prefer a particular item, but it isn't because it's not wonderfully prepared. It is guaranteed that someone will select and enjoy it. Pastoral selection is similar, except that the choices we make have far greater and longer ramifications, so we must choose wisely.

Here is a list of the pastoral leadership styles on your buffet. There may be some not included, but these are the most typical in churches. Keep in mind that all can be delicious, though some are easier to digest than others. They will all be made better when the humility factor is added to the recipe.

Positives and Negatives

As we discuss the many leadership styles and their corresponding traits, I will point out the positive and negative qualities that each style exhibits, knowing that none are all good or bad. Situational leadership scholar Paul Hersey supported this, saying, "Leadership styles or approaches can be effective or ineffective depending upon the situation."[218] The goal is to find the leader who has the right temperament, skill set, and leadership style that your church needs for the current situation, blended with the attributes of the humility factor.

Quoting the modern father of servant leadership, Greenleaf, "It is an art to drive hard with a light hand,"[219] but that is exactly what great pastoral leaders do, either by natural giftedness, surrender to the Holy Spirit's leading, or the intentional shaping of one's behavior. Scripture instructs leaders to be clothed with humility toward others, "for God opposes the proud but gives grace to the humble."[220] According to Sanders in the book *Spiritual Leadership*, "Pride ever lurks at the heels of power, but God will not encourage proud men in His service...to the undershepherd who is humble and lowly in heart, God will add power and grace to the work."[221]

Poet William Penn is quoted as stating, "Sense shines with a double luster when it is set in humility. An able yet humble man is a jewel worth a kingdom." Obviously, the view is that leading with a humble, bottom-up posture is uncommon, which Owens and Hekman support when they write, "Leader humility is still viewed as a rare personality trait that somewhat mysteriously produces favorable organizational outcomes."[222] It is unfortunate that humility is considered a rare quality in leaders, and even more so in pastors. This should not be the case, as their example is Jesus, who in every way modeled what it meant to be a leader with humble intelligence. However, as Keucher states, "Despite Jesus' example, throughout history there have certainly been Christian leaders who were arrogant, ambitious, narcissistic, and careless. Without humility, strength of character and self-confidence quickly become arrogance."[223] Deeply profound theological scholar Henri Nouwen spoke of a great irony of Christian history – the fact that leaders appear to be unable to resist the temptation and lure of power.[224] He states, "Much Christian leadership is exercised by people who do not know how to develop healthy, intimate relationships and have opted for power and control instead."[225] These are strong words of judgment towards pastors who lack humble intelligence. They have certainly turned to the dark side, which the next story illustrates. Please note that this story is a parody!

Could This Really Happen?

A regional paper reported the following:
In a shocking disaster, the stage at Faithpoint Church (fictional) suddenly collapsed right in the middle of the sermon Sunday, as the pastor's ego had grown so large the structure could no longer support his weight, sources confirmed. "The common thread through all the stories of the great heroes of the Bible is that all of them believed in themselves when the going got tough," eloquently preached the pastor as his audience of 4,000 hung on every word. "And today, I'm here to tell you that you are awesome, and that I am awesome, too! Say it with me: I

am awesome!" Smiling, the preacher said, "I hope you're paying attention, because, man, I'm preaching good!" he yelled.

As the pastor continued to declare how awesome he was, a loud crunch reportedly reverberated throughout the massive worship center. The pastor then looked around, bewildered, just moments before he plummeted through the rapidly collapsing stage, through the floor underneath the stage, and into the church's basement.

"This happens from time to time," a church architectural consultant told reporters. "Megachurch stages are required to handle up to five tons of pastoral ego, but once in a while even that's not enough."

The pastor's pride is expected to make a full recovery, according to medical experts. [226]

▲ ▲ ▲

This is a comical, but sad, account of an obviously-gifted leader who let their ego get out of control. This is then made worse by followers who feed the self-indulgence and cheer them on. Theological scholar Corne' Bekker states that "positions of power and influence have the tendency to attract the proud and upwardly mobile,"[227] which the pastor in this fictitious story illustrated. There is definitely a lure of power, influence, acclaim, and a host of perks which can draw even the most passionate about Christ to the dark side of leadership. Bonem and Patterson warn of the difficulty pastors experience when the rewards of ministry overtake one's willingness to put aside position and power in favor of picking up a towel of service.[228] Even in the secular marketplace, *Good to Great* author Jim Collins identifies personal humility as a defining factor of powerful and transformative leaders.[229]

One of the darkest temptations which pastors experience is power, particularly when they have been allowed by their lay leadership to accumulate, consolidate, and exercise it without accountability. Unrestricted power, manifest in freedom, access, influence, privilege and information,[230] may begin quite innocently, but most often leads to abuse and the temptation to act in unethical ways, if for no other reason than because there is nothing preventing it.[231] Throughout history there have been accounts of clergy abuse due to unrestricted power and access to resources. In the time of King David, it was what is now referred to by Ludwig and Longenecker as the "Bathsheba Syndrome."[232] In today's world it is simply another pastoral scandal.

Having it All, Yet Wanting More

The story of David and Bathsheba describes a leader with a humble past, a dramatic rise to power, strong organizational skills, a charismatic personality, an eclectic approach to problem-solving, a strategic vision for his people, and a man of high moral character. Yet despite both the quality of his life and his moral character, King David was a leader who got caught up in a downward spiral of unethical decisions that had grave consequences for both his personal life and the organization that he was called upon to lead and protect. A good, bright, successful, popular, visionary king, David was nearly destroyed because he could not control his desire to have something that he knew it was wrong for him to have – Bathsheba.

In short, too many of the perpetrators of the violations we witness are men and women of strong personal integrity and intelligence – men and women who have climbed the ladder through hard work and keeping their noses clean. However, just at the moment of seemingly having it all, they throw it all away by engaging in an activity that is wrong, which they know is wrong, which they know would lead to their downfall if discovered, and which they mistakenly believe they have the power to conceal.[233]

▲ ▲ ▲

Unrestricted and unaccountable power is one of the stated reasons that many people have chosen to leave the church and have nothing to do with it.[234] This casualty not only impacts the kingdom of God and the local church, but has an eternal negative consequence for the person turned off by the egotistical and tyrannical behaviors of the pastor. Everyone loses. This is why Greenleaf writes, "Absolutely no one is to be entrusted with the operational use of power without the close oversight of trustees."[235] It is imperative for your pastor to avoid the dark side; however, if they are already there, the application of the humility factor will help.

Styles and Traits

Authentic
The traits of an authentic leader are self-awareness, a clear moral perspective, discipline, relational transparency and purpose-driven focus. They are agile, adapt well to other cultures, and are able to find solutions to challenges because they are open to other people's perspectives.[236] Authentic leaders are "individuals who know who they are and what they think and are perceived by others as being aware of their own values, moral perspective, knowledge and strengths."[237] One of the true strengths of authentic leaders is that they "are presumed to be free of the need

to engage in ego-protecting biases that distort the process of self-relevant information."[238] Many 21st century leaders openly aspire to be authentic leaders.

▲ ▲ ▲

When the humility factor is added to the leadership style of **Authentic**, *the humble pastor outcome is that the leader draws people to themselves and their cause. Positive qualities are amplified, while negative qualities fall away due to heightened self-awareness and a broken and meek spirit. People trust and desire to follow this kind of leader.*

▲ ▲ ▲

Autocratic – Commanding
This leader has positional power, which means that they have power because of the position they fill. "Do it because I said so" is a common modus operandi of many "old-school" pastors. They tend to be inflexible, intimidating, unwilling to listen to others' views, and impatient, and consider questioning directives to be disloyal. Autocratic leadership, also referred to as traditional or command-and-control leadership, manifests itself by requiring their own approval of projects and activities of subordinates, centralized management, and using words such as "empowerment" to impose purpose and initiative on workers while not seeking their input.[239] Dan Kimball describes this type of leader in the statement, "Church has so many levels of hierarchy. It seems like a presidency, with the pastor being the president and wielding power over his people."[240]

It is understood that power is the currency of modern leadership and that it simply means influence by one person over others; however, contained within its dark side are the addictive properties that can overtake good leaders.[241] Staff members, lay leaders and the congregation may desire a more democratic way of doing things, but unfortunately, autocratic leaders justify their independent authority based on their divine appointment.[242] When people disagree, it is unlikely that they will influence the command-and-control leader to change their ways. Rather, they will probably leave the church. Staff members may also; however, they don't leave a bad church, but rather, in their opinion, a bad boss.[243]

According to C. S. Lewis, "Power is what pride really enjoys: there is nothing that makes a man feel so superior to others as being able to move them about like toy soldiers. It is a spiritual cancer."[244] This is why the Christian leader is directed to not be dictatorial, or to lord it over others,[245] because power is not intended to be merely a right, but also a responsibility, and the misuse will result in negative consequences. However, with all the dark side identified, it must be stated that autocratic leaders are also quite productive. They have the ability to get things done, and churches will benefit from their drive and the demand that others do as they instruct. They may be "diabolical dictators"[246] in the eyes of some, but they are effective. They also will often have the ability to draw followers to them, as the next story describes.

Have You Tried the Church Down the Street?

> The senior pastor was the quintessential command-and-control leader of a successful and growing regional church that had tripled in size since the beginning of his tenure. He had a talented and committed staff of pastors, and the culture of the church was to do things bigger, better, and best, which they were doing on a regular basis. The pastor was a gifted communicator

and an excellent administrator, though domineering in his style of leadership. Staff members knew quite well where the lines were drawn and that questioning the decisions made by the pastor was a risky activity. At the same time, the pastor took very good care of the staff when it came to salary, benefits, and other employee perks. The pastor often referred to his style of leadership as a "benevolent dictatorship" and both words of that description were true.[247] The ministries of the church were well funded, the facilities were expansive and well equipped, and everyone was encouraged to do great things. The one true litmus test for any new idea was "Will it bring people to Jesus?"

It sounds as if it were heaven on earth, and it was, unless you opposed the pastor in any way, at which time the pastor's benevolence came to a halt. Even when an employee would play the "I believe God wants me to do this" card, the pastor's answer would often be, "When God starts signing your paycheck, you can do what He tells you to do. Until then you will do it my way," said with a smile, of course. Unfortunately the pastor's behavior became darker if a staff member persisted, warning, "If you oppose me, you will lose." To congregation members who raised their concern over how things were being handled, it was not unusual for the pastor to say, "You know there is a really good church down the street. Have you tried them?" said with a smile, of course.

The command-and-control leader eventually retired, passing the baton to an equally dominant leader. The church is successful, but continues to be led with an iron fist.

▲ ▲ ▲

*When the humility factor is added to the leadership style of **Autocratic-Command-and-Control**, the humble pastor outcome is that the leader becomes a strong, effective leader balanced by gentleness and compassion and open to the ideas and opinions of others. They still have some commanding qualities, but people will be willing to fall in line behind this leader as the pastor validates them.*

▲ ▲ ▲

Charismatic
The charismatic leader has the ability to inspire, motivate, or coerce people to action. They possess excellent communication skills, enjoy a bigger-than-life personality, and have abundant charm, which makes them the life of the party. People naturally gravitate to them. Charismatic pastors are attractive figures to whom people respond, and are thus able to motivate people to help the church because they believe in and admire the pastor.[248] In many cases, though, churches that are led by charismatic pastors tend to place their focus on the person of the pastor before the mission of the church. Keucher warns of this dark trait because "the moment a leader allows himself to become the primary reality people worry about, it is a recipe for mediocrity or worse."[249] Another negative is that because of the pastor's charm, coercion often becomes the standard practice to get their way. Churches of all shapes and sizes can have charismatic leaders.

▲ ▲ ▲

*When the humility factor is added to the leadership style of **Charismatic**, the humble pastor outcome is that the leader inspires others and keeps their talent for influencing* *others under control through sacrificial service to others. They are able to avoid the negative qualities of coercion and manipulation often found in this kind of leader.*

▲ ▲ ▲

Coaching

Leaders who excel at coaching are able to help others find solutions through their skill of asking great questions and being a great listener. Pastors who are coaches will be great at empowering others to do the work of ministry, though some critics may wonder what the pastor is doing personally. These pastors are highly relational, great team builders, and excellent at recruiting volunteers.

▲ ▲ ▲

*When the humility factor is added to the leadership style of **Coaching**, the humble pastor outcome is that the leader continually learns from their interaction with those they coach. They become better leaders as they see qualities in others which need to be improved in themselves. Eventually followers see their coach modeling the kind of self-improvement they are being asked to undertake and desire to follow them on the journey.*

▲ ▲ ▲

Cross-Cultural

The cross-cultural leader has an understanding of various cultures and is tolerant, open, accepting, and agile. They know that the absence of ego awareness and balance becomes an invisible boundary and creates barriers to effective partnerships in many cultures.[250] When this happens, opportunities for connection are lost, which is particularly hard for churches desiring to make a positive impact in their community.[251] This type of leader is extremely valuable to churches within a mixed-cultural demographic. The following true story further demonstrates the importance of humility when dealing with cultural borders.

Be Nice to the Guards

> As part of a 94-member American teenage band and drill team, I traveled throughout Europe in two large buses and an equipment truck. I remember that the guards at the borders took their jobs very seriously as they questioned the leaders in each vehicle making the crossing from one country to another. Our director, whom many considered a benevolent dictator with a love for people, especially teenagers, was very clear about how we were supposed to behave: keep our conversations quiet, and under no circumstances take the situation lightly by cracking a joke or being disrespectful in any way to the guards, who had the authority to detain us from getting to our next concert. Our purpose for being halfway around the world was to entertain and serve as ambassadors of music from the United States, and the expectation was that we would display a gracious and humble attitude to all with whom we came in contact, including the guards at the checkpoints. Any display of hubris would only reinforce what many Europeans already thought about Americans – that we were cocky, overly self-assured, and believed that our country's ways were superior to other countries' cultures and ways of doing things. Our demeanor at border crossings needed to be the polar opposite, otherwise, our trip

of goodwill would turn south very quickly. Fortunately, everyone behaved themselves (even the drummers), and we were able to navigate through seven countries and perform 23 concerts and a parade in 21 days.

⋏ ⋏ ⋏

It is reported that Pope Francis regularly calls for church leaders to be "ministers of mercy above all" and has laid out an ambitious vision for the church, stating,

> I dream of a church that is a mother and a shepherdess. The church ministers must be merciful, take responsibility for the people and accompany them like the Good Samaritan, who washes, cleans and raises up his neighbor. This is pure Gospel.[252]

The words of Pope Francis speak to the biblical mandate that churches have been given to put aside personal agenda, comfort, and status in favor of coming to the aid of the community in which they reside and other cultures, regardless of the boundaries that exist. To do so, leaders cannot begin from a mindset of superiority and hubris, but rather as humble servants. Standish writes, "Humble leaders let Christ lead through them, guiding people to follow God's path."[253]

Imagine the difference it would make in the eyes of the community if cross-cultural church leaders demonstrated that they thought no more of themselves than of the people they were trying to reach; if, instead of coming across as a superior group of people reaching down to help the downtrodden, they came alongside equally flawed fellow human beings who were sharing the journey with them. For churches and their leaders to break through the boundaries that separate people from one another, they must follow Christ's example of taking on the role of a servant by picking up a towel and basin in order to wash the feet of friends, neighbors, strangers, and even those who might wish them harm.[254]

▲ ▲ ▲

When the humility factor is added to the leadership style of **Cross-Cultural**, *the humble pastor outcome is that the leader has a greater ability to see cultures and individuals through a new lens of acceptance, understanding, and compassion. This is appealing to not only followers on the home front, but others whose context of culture is entirely different. When they perceive the leader's openness, they feel free to develop a trusting relationship with them.*

▲ ▲ ▲

Democratic-Participative
This leader creates and uses a safe environment to make group decisions through discussion. They have excellent listening and delegation skills, a team orientation, and a belief that everyone is valuable. It is important that the democratic leader be comfortable in their own skin and without a fragile ego that can be threatened by others on the team.[255] My observation is that there are not many democratic-participative leaders in lead pastor roles.

▲ ▲ ▲

When the humility factor is added to the leadership style of **Democratic-Participative**, *the humble pastor outcome is that the leader becomes a collaborative leader with a high level of emotional intelligence and healthy, open* *relationships among team members. They model forgiveness, gratitude, compassion, and service, all qualities which others will desire to emulate.*

Foresight

The foresight leader is future-thinking, innovative, open, entrepreneurial, and an opportunist who bases their projections on scientific analysis. Churches with a foresight leader will be exciting and a little bit scary. These leaders must make sure that they communicate well and invest in relationships with the movers and shakers of the church. Buy-in by the lay leaders will be particularly important as the foresight leader describes the future that they see as possible for the church, as it will involve both evolutionary (continuous) and revolutionary (radical) change initiatives.[256] Another reason relationships are critical is that many people will not immediately have the ability to see into the future as the leader does. They will need to fully trust their pastor not to lead them astray while in the midst of great uncertainty.

*When the humility factor is added to the leadership style of **Foresight**, the humble pastor outcome is that the all-about-the-future leader becomes grounded in the present through the development of solid relationships. People will admire the vision and imagination of the leader while respecting the down-to-earth understanding about living in the real world that their leader has.*

Humble

A humble leader is collaborative, thinks higher of others than themselves, shares decisions and authority, gives away credit, and is self-aware. According to *Eats with Sinners* author Arron Chambers, the essence of humility begins at the foot of the cross[257] and the willingness to do whatever is necessary to save another person from an eternity without God. Using a well into which people have fallen as a metaphor for those who have fallen into sin, Chambers states,

> Christlike humility requires that we never forget the well and those trapped inside it. None of us is too good, too holy, too important, too successful, too prominent in our denomination, too valuable to our church board, too recognizable from our television ministry, too anything to help hurting people out of the well.[258]

Standish simply states that "humility is a way of life in which we [pastors] become consumed with seeking God's direction rather than living purely according to our instincts, conditioning, and insights,"[259] and St. Augustine is quoted as stating, "Should you ask me: What is the first thing in religion? I should reply: The first, second, and third thing therein is humility."[260] Remember our premise – healthy churches are led by humble pastors.

▲ ▲ ▲

Purpose-Driven Leader

A fantastic example of a humble leader is Pastor Rick Warren, the founding pastor of Saddleback Church in Southern California and the author of the bestselling book *The Purpose Driven Life*. It would be reasonable to expect that someone with his credentials might be less humble than he displays. His accomplishments are great and he has literally changed how churches function and, through his books, changed countless lives in a positive direction. Churches all over the world have participated in the various 40 Days programs which he began, so honestly, he has a right to be at least a little proud of the things he's done. However, his published bio reads, "No socks. Loves Jesus. Mentors young leaders. Helps the sick and poor. Serves Saddleback. Encourages pastors. Wrote some books." There is no mention of the magnitude of his impact on the church and the world, just simple phrases that say what he does and has done. Pastor Warren is a living example of a gifted pastor who has experienced how the attributes of the humility factor change the way you lead, and his church continues to benefit from his humble leadership style.

▲ ▲ ▲

*When the humility factor is added to the leadership style of **Humble**, the humble pastor outcome is that the leader becomes a better version of themselves and, due to their broken spirit, resists the tendency to become proud of their humility. People may not realize exactly what draws them to their leader, but they will desire to be around them and follow their lead.*

▲ ▲ ▲

Laissez-Faire
This type of leader uses delegation and hands-off supervision when dealing with staff, lay leaders and volunteers. Though this may be a style in an established church that has many structures

and practices in place, the lead may be considered disengaged and dispassionate. A church can function with a laissez-faire leader for a short time and remain moderately effective; however, for long-term growth, this style of leadership will become too casual an approach and people will fade away as they find another church and leader that they perceive as more exciting.

▲ ▲ ▲

When the humility factor is added to the leadership style of **Laissez-Faire**, *the humble pastor outcome is that, while keeping their laid-back approach to management, this leader becomes highly relational and quietly serves others on the team. Followers may still desire a more dynamic approach, but will appreciate the fact that their leader cares for them.*

▲ ▲ ▲

Narcissistic
Let's begin by identifying the potentially positive results that can come from a church having a pastor who is a narcissist. Yes, there really are some. We will spend a little extra time with this leadership style both because there is a vast amount written about it, and simply because, sadly, so many churches' lead pastors exhibit these behaviors. According to author Elizabeth Lunbeck, "Healthy narcissism can help you succeed!"[261] as these individuals appear empathetic, engaging, determined, and wise in such a way that they appeal similar to "a modern-day Sir Lancelot, replete with the most swaggering charm one could imagine and adorned in the shining armor of our time: a handsome portfolio and dazzling acquisitions."[262] Even Pastor Standish agrees that there can be a healthy version of a

narcissist when they are aware of their self-absorption and are actively working on humility. They can be very good at leading large organizations partly due to their natural ability to lead, and because the size of their church allows them to avoid intimate relationships.[263] They will do whatever they need to do to make their church successful because their ethical egoism demands that they maximize their own benefits,[264] and it allows them to satisfy their drive for symbolic immortality and legacy creation.[265]

Unfortunately, there is a dominant dark side to narcissistic leadership. Keeping in mind the positive image of Sir Lancelot above, in the book *Disarming the Narcissist*, the author completes the description stating,

> Beware! This knight is a master of illusion. In fact, he can be downright menacing. You may fall prey to the seductive lure of his accomplishments, intelligence, and seemingly flawless self-confidence. However, his arrogance, condescension, sense of entitlement, and lack of empathy are formidable offenders that inevitably lead to frustrating interpersonal encounters and chronically difficult long-term relationships.[266]

When a congregation lavishes admiration and rewards on a pastor who is a narcissist, they do so at the risk of great peril,[267] because once in power, these leaders will feel entitled to satisfy their desires, even at the expense of others.[268] They become toxic to their church[269] as they operate with an overblown sense of self-worth and self-interest, abusing power and manipulating subordinates for their personal gain, often without knowing what they are doing.[270] Taking advantage of others becomes second nature to them and they truly believe their own lies.[271] The prophet Obadiah spoke of them, saying, "The pride of your heart has deceived you, you who live in the clefts of the rock, in your lofty dwelling, who say in your heart, 'Who will bring me down to the ground?'"[272]

Summarizing much of the research that has been done, narcissism is a preoccupation with one's own self-importance and the belief that one is special and more important than others. Narcissists have arrogant fantasies of endless success, a hypersensitivity to criticism, and a lack of empathy, plus being exploitative of others and operating with an extreme sense of entitlement, including the need to be the center of attention. Though often charming, they can also be cold, ruthless and controlling, all the while oblivious to their behavior.[273] They are threatened by others' success, reward only those who benefit them, have difficulty sharing, are generous only when it makes them look good, and have situational ethics. As Engstrom discusses in his classic book, *The Making of a Christian Leader*, their self-esteem is so weak that their behavior is much like that of a playground bully who abuses others in order to feel better about himself.[274]

I recently came across a poem of an unknown origin. It is a haunting example of the prayer of a narcissist. Here is an excerpt.

It's All About ME
Oh Mesus
Know this is for me, for my comfort and my vain.
It's not about YOU as if I should do things YOUR way.
You alone are God, but I surrender to no one.
Mesus, lover of myself
All consumerism is in my gaze
Mesus, I want thee to know,
I will please myself all of my days.[275]

A few years back I wrote an article to prompt church lay leaders to ask themselves if their senior pastor was a narcissist. Here are some of those thoughts to ask yourselves now.

Your Senior Pastor Might Be a Narcissist if...

> If they have little or no regard for staff members' time and schedule, your senior pastor might be a narcissist. If they openly admit that they "don't share well" when it comes to support staff and resources, your senior pastor might be a narcissist. If they attempt to dissolve the executive board of the church and state that they are "the man of God whose decisions must not be questioned," they might be a narcissist. If they insist that their picture be included on all church literature and even a public billboard, and state, "I want to be the show" when planning a major holiday service, they might be a narcissist. When the best way to get a new idea accepted is to show how they'll personally have greater exposure and people will think higher of them, they might be a narcissist. When loyalty only goes one way, they do all of the talking, they are threatened by the success of their team members, and their behavior is inconsistent with their words, they might definitely be a narcissist![276]

▲ ▲ ▲

*When the humility factor is added to the leadership style of **Narcissistic**, the humble pastor outcome is that the leader, through new awareness and brokenness, begins the difficult journey to learn to think of others before they* *naturally and habitually think of themselves. This will also be greatly helped by the leader's intentionally and anonymously serving others. People will follow this leader because they see an effort to change and become a better, less self-focused leader.*

▲ ▲ ▲

Pacesetting

A pacesetting leader gives high energy to achieving, moving so fast it is difficult for others to keep up, and is highly critical of those who aren't as driven to succeed. They have unreasonable expectations of employees. This is what the research of emotional intelligence classifies as a dissonant leadership style, though it can be effective, providing that the employees are self-motivated, driven, and highly talented. Unfortunately, even when people are those things, they may still respond poorly to a pacesetting boss. Due to the fact that they push so hard and expect so much, the employee actually closes themselves to them and morale plummets.

> According to the work of Goleman,
> The leader holds and exemplifies high standards for performance. He is obsessive about doing things better and faster, and asks the same of everyone. He quickly pinpoints poor performers, demands more from them, and if they don't rise to the occasion, rescues the situation himself. But if applied poorly or excessively, or in the wrong setting, the pacesetting approach can leave employees feeling pushed too hard by the leader's relentless demands.[277]

Pacesetting often is the result of a leader's lack of self-awareness, which leaves them blind to their own failings[278] even as they point out the shortcomings of their team members. This lack is responsible for many pacesetting leaders not having healthy humility.[279] Unfortunately, the pacesetting style most often does not lead to a happy ending, which the following story will show.

It Was My Fault

>A while back I was serving a large and effective church. I was the long-term worship pastor and part of the executive staff. We had grown exponentially and relocated to a great new facility, and with it, the worship ministry was strong, gifted, and doing some wonderful work. I was a driven, focused, and pacesetting leader. I knew what I wanted us to accomplish and I tried my best to model the passion, energy, and effort which I desired each of my team members to also display. My team worked hard and we presented excellent and consistent worship services and over-the-top seasonal events that brought in large crowds. We really had things going, and these accomplishments are examples of how the pacesetting style can make great things happen.
>
>Unfortunately, there was a dark side to which I was completely blind. I had a fantastic team of talented worship artists who were accomplished, creative, committed, and a load of fun. There was never a time where I didn't enjoy the time we worked side by side in our ministry. Did I say fun? This group was off-the-charts fun. The problem was that I was so driven to be bigger, better, and best at what we did together, I forgot the fun part, and the empathetic part, and the people-are-more- important-than-work part. I was a classic pacesetter. It's not that I didn't think my team members were doing a great job, because

I knew they were, but I was over-driven to succeed and I would move as fast as I could to do more, in less time, and bigger and better than anyone else.

If it had only been me pushing myself to function at that frenetic pace, that might have been okay, but I pushed everyone to do the same. When they didn't, I got frustrated with them and I pushed harder. Gradually each of the team members started to avoid me and the tension in the office was unbearable. I had lost the hearts of my team and it was my fault. Eventually, many of them left for better working conditions. One of my greatest regrets is that I pushed wonderful people into leaving what should have been a heaven-on-earth ministry environment. I wish I could go back and do it differently.

The entire experience still puts a knot in my stomach, but there are several good things that have come out of it. Soon after things began to fall apart, I learned about the pacesetting style. When I first read the description, I was struck with the truth that it was describing me. Going through it all also helped me to take some early steps in my humility journey, which I described in detail in chapter two. The best thing is that I am a different person and a different leader today. Since then, I have tried to make up with each of the team members who had to endure my pacesetting style. It's still a work in progress, but I want them to know that I am sorry for being that kind of leader. Now, when I am consulting with pastors, if I see the evidence of pacesetting, I tell them my story in the hope that I'll help them to change their ways and keep the good people they have on their team.

▲ ▲ ▲

*When the humility factor is added to the leadership style of **Pacesetting**, the humble pastor outcome is that self-awareness and openness will alert this leader to their tendency to push too hard and expect too much, hopefully before their followers quit. However, it may take losing good people in order to bring about a brokenness that will lead to a less-driving manner of leadership. Eventually, however, they may become someone whom many are willing and eager to follow.*

▲ ▲ ▲

Pharisee
This isn't a leadership style that is talked about much these days, but unfortunately, there are still Pharisees in our organizations, and especially in our churches, who, due to their self-righteous pride and judgmentalism, are driving many people away from the church.[280] In a nutshell, the Pharisee leadership style is all about self-righteousness. In the book *Hope in Troubled Times*, the discussion is about how ideologies are at the core of self-righteousness and that this style does not embrace wisdom, but rather foolishness.[281] One of the reasons people are repelled by judgmental pastors is because in the 21st century, just as in the time of Christ, a Pharisee is seen as self-righteous, hypocritical, and one who takes pride in "behaving in a very correct and proper way and who felt morally superior to people who followed more relaxed standards."[282] This description is very much in line with how the Pharisees of Jesus' day acted and for whom He saved his harshest judgment. Jesus spoke to the crowds and to his disciples about how the Pharisees would "tie up heavy burdens, hard to bear, and lay them on people's shoulders,"[283] meaning that they piled on extreme requirements to fulfill the law far beyond what anyone could actually accomplish, making people feel unworthy of God

and further strengthening the Pharisee's position of spiritual authority and power.

Modern-day Pharisees are the pastors who set spiritual standards high, to unbelievable and often unattainable heights. They preach a narrow line that is without grace and filled with guilt. They speak with the authority of scripture, yet without compassion, and with the pride of a tyrannical commander[284] who believes that they know best what everyone should do in all circumstances. This leader is legalistic, arrogant, uncaring, and relationally deficient. They are egotists who believe the ends justify the means and that they are the only ones to whom God speaks, thus they deserve to make and enforce the rules and to be held in honor. Pharisees have the potential to call people to raise the bar when it comes to following Christ; however, all too often in doing so, they make people feel that they are too unworthy to even try. Again from *Hope in Troubled Times*, "Under no circumstances may Christians claim at the outset that they possess better insights than others, nor do they have the right to equate their own partial insights with the unique message of the gospel itself."[285] Pharisees are all about the rules to which they feel everyone should adhere. Like their command-and-control counterparts, it's their way or the highway, which the next story demonstrates.

If They Leave, So Be It

> One of the hallmarks of a Pharisee is that they will tell people how they should live. No discussion. No questions. No possibility that there might be another perspective or way of doing things. To the Pharisee, they are right and everyone should do as they say. This was the case of a Pharisee-type pastor who was in line to

succeed the previous pastor and become the new lead. The church had done well, and over a long time frame had developed a wide variety of activities, programs, events, and more, including many serving ministries which brought together people of similar interests to do specific forms of service. The church, though dealing with some plateau issues, which is not unusual in an established church, was not failing, though it needed a few kicks in its backside to get some things moving again. The soon-to-be pastor, having read the latest trendy, but unsubstantiated and biased, book on how to overcome the status quo, came up with a plan that he was convinced the church for which he would soon be calling all the shots, must adopt. He presented his plan to the staff with the instruction from the outgoing command-and-control pastor to make it happen. No discussion. No questions. No possibility that there might be another perspective or way of doing things. Questions were viewed as resistance and the person asking them was labeled as standing in the way of the future pastor.

The way this was handled was riddled with problems related to the command-and-control and dictatorial nature of the outgoing pastor, but what made this a matter of a Pharisee leadership style is that once the plan was developed, it was presented to the congregation as the only way someone could remain in good grace at the church. The statement by the incoming pastor was, "If you want to be a fully devoted follower of Christ at this church, you must do these things." Groups, activities, events, and long-standing and loved traditions were disposed of in favor of the things on the approved list. Some members left the church hurt and insulted, feeling that the Pharisee pastor was out of line to question their commitment to Christ simply because they didn't do things exactly as he said they must. Others stuck around, but remain deeply disappointed that some of the things which made the church special to them had been taken away. Relationships were broken and long-term members of the church and staff left, feeling pushed out and discarded. The Pharisee had spoken. Everyone must get in line. When asked if it bothered him that people were leaving over his legalistic policies, he defiantly and callously replied, "If they leave, so be it!"

▲ ▲ ▲

While I hope that the Pharisee pastor has mellowed with age, I believe it is possible that they still conduct themselves with the same cavalier attitude, partially due to their passionate belief that they are right and partially because they are allowed to behave in this way by their hand-picked board members.

▲ ▲ ▲

When the humility factor is added to the leadership style of **Pharisee**, *the humble pastor outcome is that the development of compassion, forgiveness, and openness will occur. Once in place, this leader will be able to continue to uphold high standards, but do so with a softer, loving touch. Followers will respect the conviction of their leader, however, not feel put down by them when they either don't agree or fail to meet the standards set.*

▲ ▲ ▲

Resonant

Resonant leaders are all about people. They have excellent skills to powerfully, passionately, and purposefully move people in positive directions that will benefit their families, organizations, and communities.[286] When working with individuals and groups, they are able to make deep emotional connections and inspire them to do their best work, raise their standards, and be a better version of themselves. Simply put, they bring out the best in people.

A resonant leader has emotional intelligence and the five personal competencies of self-awareness, emotion management, self-motivation, empathy, and relational management.[287] They also have a heightened social awareness that allows them to see and meet the needs of people inside and outside their church walls. Resonant leaders are the polar opposite of dissonant leaders, such as the pacesetter described above. In the words of the 21st century management consultant Ronald Watson, "Resonant leaders have the ability to maintain harmonious, productive relationships with those around them, even as workload and stress increase."[288] Churches with resonant leaders, particularly when their positive traits are mixed with the humility factor, will be healthy places to worship, serve, and work.

▲ ▲ ▲

When the humility factor is added to the leadership style of ***Resonant****, the humble pastor outcome is that all qualities of the leader will be enhanced as they increase their service to others with an emerging broken will. People will want to sign up to be on this leader's team because they trust them and believe in their vision of the future.*

▲ ▲ ▲

Selfless
There are three defining characteristics of a selfless leader. They:

- Sacrifice for the benefit of others
- Give the spotlight to others
- Always encourage others

Selfless leaders are those who make personal and professional sacrifices for the good of their mission, their organization, their team, and the people they serve. Sacrificing for the benefit of others is their standard practice and a part of their DNA.

Although a selfless leader may be highly gifted and attract attention, they don't overtly seek the spotlight and are always on the lookout for opportunities to elevate others, knowing that when their team succeeds, so do they. Selfless leaders refuse to be insecure when those around them do well, and they are confident within their own skin, even when surrounded by highly gifted people.

Selfless leaders always encourage their team members, whether in private, publicly, face-to-face, electronically, or through social media. They understand that a key requirement for keeping great people is that they know that they are wanted, respected, and valued by their leader.[289]

▲ ▲ ▲

When the humility factor is added to the leadership style of **Selfless***, the humble pastor outcome is that the leader's qualities of compassion, gratitude, and forgiveness will emerge through their growing awareness of brokenness. People will enjoy serving alongside their leader because of the sacrificial service that is modeled, the shared spotlight, and the continual encouragement given.*

▲ ▲ ▲

Servant

The essence of servant leadership is that the leader's primary aim is to serve their followers. This motivation is based on what Greenleaf calls the conscious choice to lead, yet is guided by the choice to be a servant first.[290] "Servant leaders provide vision, gain credibility and trust from followers and influence others by focusing on bringing out the best in their followers."[291]

Humility evidences itself particularly well in servant leadership, in which Jesus serves as the quintessential example.[292] In 1 Corinthians 12, Paul expounds on how one part of the body of Christ is no greater than another, how all parts are necessary, and that those thought of as lesser will be given greater honor.[293] In the book of Philippians, Paul writes, "Do nothing from selfish ambition or conceit, but in humility count others more significantly than yourselves."[294] Servant leadership in its purest form is the combination of humble intelligence and putting others' needs ahead of one's own, both of which lead to unity within the church and the greater body of Christ. It begins with the leader, who models humility for the rest of the team and potentially "opens up magnanimity to gratitude, delight, and wonder at God's creation."[295] Standish adds, "Humility is the willingness to become God- and other-focused rather than being narcissistically self-focused. It's becoming a servant of God and others."[296] The following story is one which I will never forget and I use as an example often. The person was not a pastor, but very easily could have been.

The Glamour Part of the Job

> My wife and I were exhibiting for the first time at a national music and worship conference, where we had dramatic materials available for churches to use in their worship arts ministries. I spent most of the week teaching workshops and attending music reading sessions while Karen served

in the booth, talking with people, developing relationships, selling materials, and being her typical ambassador of goodwill. Since this was our first time at this conference (in which we subsequently participated for the next 21 years), we made an effort to get to know the other exhibitors who were part of the gospel music industry and with whom we were hoping to build partnerships. Our booth was small and our exhibit very modest, but we were there to get started, so we got right to work as the conference opened.

Next to us was a multi-space exhibit featuring one of the larger music distributors in the industry. There were several people who worked the conference with whom we became friendly. We shared our snacks and chatted with them throughout the week. It was a good week and a great learning experience for us. When the conference was coming to a close and the exhibits were being shut down, all of us in the exhibit hall began to pack up our materials and furnishings from the booths, including our new friends in the booth next to us. As we said goodbye, we exchanged business cards. I put them in my pocket and didn't take another look until we got home and I sat down to write follow-up notes to everyone I had met at the conference. When I got to our booth neighbors, I was stunned to see that one of the people we had gotten to know the most while working the exhibit, including set up and tear down, was the president of the company. I was impressed that he did the grunt work alongside his staff.

A few months later we saw the same group at another conference. Once again, I watched the president of the company unpack materials, answer countless questions, and when it was all over, take off his tie, roll up his sleeves and get to the dusty work of packing up. At this point, we had become somewhat friends and I told him how impressed I was that even though he was the big boss, he was doing the dirty work with everyone else. Without a moment of hesitation, he stated, "This is the glamour part of the job." I know now that I was in the presence of a true servant leader. He was not going to ask his team to do something that he wasn't willing to do himself, or at least to help with. I observed this servant leader consistently serve others for the next couple of decades, and I have tried to follow his model and emulate his ways.

⸪

When the humility factor is added to the leadership style of **Servant***, the humble pastor outcome is that the leader's heightened self-awareness and brokenness will complete the package of a leader who considers others' needs before their own. The others will, in turn, desire to be a servant as well, which will cause the organization to take on the same qualities, resulting in a servant serving servants who serve their community for maximum positive impact.*

⸪

Shepherd
A shepherd leader is highly relational and prefers to spend the majority of their time with the people they serve, rather than doing administrative tasks. Just as the name implies, they are happiest when they are hanging out with their sheep! They are caring and empathetic, and good counselors who will help others through their challenges and make them feel loved. They understand that sometimes sheep go astray, and they will go out of their way to bring them back to the flock with grace and care, and when

necessary, correct the behavior of a member of the flock with a loving swat with their shepherd's staff. The shepherd leader is generally a positive style, but they must be careful of the influence which they will develop as people are drawn to them. Nouwen warned pastors that "shepherding quickly becomes a subtle way of exercising power over others and begins to show authoritarian and dictatorial traits."[297] The key to a shepherd avoiding the lure of this level of influence is to remain self-aware, grateful, and open to the input of others.

▲ ▲ ▲

When the humility factor is added to the leadership style of **Shepherd**, the humble pastor outcome is that every quality of the humility factor already within the shepherd will be enhanced, benefiting both the shepherd and the members of the flock. People will follow this leader because of the care they receive from them, however, sometimes caution must be observed so that people are not following blindly. Assessment and accountability must be ongoing as to the intentions and objectives of this leader.

▲ ▲ ▲

Situational
In many ways, the situational leader is the best of all worlds for a church because of their ability to assess changing circumstances and adjust their methods according to changing needs. Too often strong pastors struggle to switch their practices to match needs and miss opportunities as they present themselves. The situational leader is agile, analytical, a strong decision-maker, and open. They react quickly to opportunities and challenges with confidence and a spirit of optimism. They believe that they can

overcome whatever is thrown at them because they have a large toolbox of techniques from which to choose. The downside of a situational leader can be the perception that they flip flop on issues that lay leaders may think have been settled. Because this leader is willing to stay open to options, they may frustrate those who are ready to move in the particular direction decided upon.

▲ ▲ ▲

When the humility factor is added to the leadership style of **Situational***, the humble pastor outcome is that the softer skills related to relationships will make this decisive leader more approachable. People will trust their leader's judgment as a track record of success develops, and there will be an affirmative acceptance that the leader won't use the same tactics for every circumstance.*

▲ ▲ ▲

Strategic
This leader is a long-term thinker, analytical, decisive, and action- and results-oriented. They work well in situations in which the church is ready to make changes in their plans for long-term community impact, such as moving from a neighborhood church to a high-visibility regional location, or the changing of the culture from an inward "take care of our members" focus to an outreach "let's be the hands and feet of Jesus to our community" focus. The results orientation of the strategic leader will help the church gain stature, recognition, reputation, and influence in the community, but can also put pressure on the staff to perform at levels higher than they may be accustomed to or able to attain. The strategic leader must also be self-aware enough to recognize that they can be more task-oriented than people-oriented and that sometimes

they are insensitive to the human needs of today because they are so laser-focused on tomorrow.

▲ ▲ ▲

When the humility factor is added to the leadership style of **Strategic**, *the humble pastor outcome is similar to that of situational leaders, in which the softer skills will make the relational aspect of leading a team better for everyone. People will appreciate the in-depth planning and execution of the leader while being grateful that they are led by someone who takes the time to see them as a person first and a part of the organizational machine second.*

▲ ▲ ▲

Transactional

The underlying practice of transactional leadership is an "I will do this if you will do that" contract between a leader and their followers. It has its roots in the old-school attitude of leaders that employees aren't inherently self-motivated to do good work, so it is necessary to promise an enticement or punishment to make people want to work hard.[298] This, of course, is the negative approach to what can be a mutually-beneficial arrangement between managers and employees. Modern transactional leaders are goal- and rewards-oriented and results-driven within a reciprocal relational context. They have good negotiation skills and the desire to attain satisfaction on both sides of the employee contract. The setting of objectives, monitoring and controlling outcomes is still part of a positive transactional relationship,[299] but caution must be observed so that followers don't feel that they are outranked by their leader, even if they are. It's important that everyone plays by the same rules. In the best-case scenarios, all parties feel that they are a valuable part of the effort which is performed by different, but equal participants, avoiding what Standish called "social Darwinism," in which only the strongest deserve to rule.[300]

Transactional leadership can be a positive experience between the pastor and the people who mutually agree to objectives and goals, methods and practices, and rewards for everyone who contributed to the successful collaborative effort. Unfortunately, this type of leadership can fall back into the negative attitudes of its roots described in the next story.

With Rank Comes Privilege

"With rank comes privilege" was the statement made in an executive staff meeting of a large church after a discussion as to how subordinates were to proceed with a directive which clearly had one set of rules for the lower rung of the leadership ladder and another for the upper. The department heads, who reported to the executive staff, were to follow policies for the good of the organization from which their supervisors were exempt. After a question was raised regarding the fairness of such a directive, the above statement was made. Then, four of five executive staff members agreed, and the meeting proceeded by ordering lunch. This is only one example of how this church, although filled with a common sense of mission and a celebrated and lengthy track record of content staff and constituents, displayed the traits of an old-school bureaucratic management style in which directives were to be followed if one was to expect continued employment. This style, long used by the top executive of the church, caused a growing, underlying frustration and an inability for many to function in a psychologically-safe environment. Because of this, there developed a lack of intellectual, emotional, and creative freedom. This was transactional leadership at its worst. It continued until the leader retired.

▲ ▲ ▲

*When the humility factor is added to the leadership style of **Transactional**, the humble pastor outcome is that self-awareness and brokenness will provide the leader a gentler approach to achievement. They will still have a contractual approach to leader-follower relations, however, they will manage with greater empathy and a softer touch.*

▲ ▲ ▲

Transformational
This leader has the ability to convince others to be a part of organizational change and inspire them to a higher level of commitment, empowering them to do the work through their motivational lives. Transformational leaders:

- Challenge the status quo
- Articulate a compelling vision of the future
- Engage in behaviors that build followers' trust
- Listen to followers' needs and concerns
- Motivate people to achieve collective goals[301]

Transformational leaders have an uncanny ability to encourage people to rise above self-interest,[302] guide people to change their beliefs and aspirations so that they are in alignment with the pastor's vision for the church,[303] and create a mission culture built upon a strong relational foundation.[304]

▲ ▲ ▲

> When the humility factor is added to the leadership style of **Transformational**, the humble pastor outcome is that brokenness and compassion will help this leader to keep their ego in check as they become successful and effective. People will naturally want to follow this leader because people want to be a part of a winning team, but they will appreciate the personal care they receive from a coach who cares for their team members.

▲ ▲ ▲

Visionary

Visionary leaders are people-oriented, creative, and goal-oriented. They are dreamers with the ability to transform ideas into reality. Often, as is the case in the following example, visionary leadership and transformational leadership styles can be found in the same person, each enhancing the other. When a leader is merely a visionary, they may run into difficulties getting their visions to become a reality. However, when the skills associated with transformational leadership are combined with visionary leadership, visions become plans of action that can be articulated, motivated in others, and put into action.

▲ ▲ ▲

For People Who Don't Like Church

> One of the best examples I have of pastors who possess the combination of transformational and visionary leadership and display the signs of the humility factor is Ray Johnston, the founding pastor of Bayside Church in Northern California. I've known Ray for over twenty years, and looking back, virtually everything which he talked about wanting to create in a church has become a reality.

I remember times when we served together before he began Bayside that he would talk about the church which he envisioned, what its values would be, how it would function, and the impact it would have. I believed him then, though I had a bit of cautious reservation about how the whole thing would come together, but today Bayside is a phenomenal church in which tens of thousands attend worship each week in twenty services on five campuses (with more to come). It's home to some of the best church leadership conferences in the world, and Ray is connected to highly-respected pastors and causes that are household names in the church world. He is a highly effective and successful pastor.

Bayside began very humbly, but with a pastor who had a vision that wouldn't stop. He began by preaching on a stage made of plywood and milk crates to people who were curious about a church that advertised, "We're the church for people who don't like church." The attendance exploded as Ray brought on talented staff members to work alongside him in a church with passionate worship, in-depth Bible teaching, unleashed compassion, and a focus on children's ministry that kids absolutely love. Today they have awesome facilities, a world-class staff, unbelievable worship artists, blow-your-mind programming, the best-mobilized volunteers I've ever seen, and about the best teaching team you could ever find, but Ray never forgets his humble beginnings at Bayside and his roots as a kid growing up in a non-Christian family.

It would be easy for someone who has accomplished so much to let it go to his head, but that's not Ray. He is a true transformational and visionary pastor, but he's also a servant and selfless leader who shares the lead pastor responsibilities with three other senior pastors and scores of other preachers. When Ray is not on the platform or ministering elsewhere in the world, you can bet he's at Bayside. He makes himself available to people and he is always challenging people to be generous and compassionate. There are a few pastors who I believe have achieved complete humble intelligence, and Ray Johnston is one of them. Bayside continues to grow and is quite certainly successful, effective, and healthy, all because it is led by a humble pastor.

▲ ▲ ▲

When the humility factor is added to the leadership style of **Visionary***, the humble pastor outcome is that, in a manner similar to transformational leaders, brokenness and self-awareness will remind this successful leader that life is not merely about them and what they can achieve. They will develop the ability to look into the future while still keeping a firm grasp of the reality of the present. From a spiritual standpoint, they will not be so heavenly minded that they are no earthly good.*

▲ ▲ ▲

Zealot
There is one final leadership style to discuss that is rooted in ambition and arrogance and carried out in haste with a lack of prudence. It should be acknowledged, though, that zealot leaders most often don't begin their ministry as a zealot. They answer the call to "preach the word"[305] and muster the courage and focus their passion to take on the mantle of leadership in a church. They, like John the Baptist proclaiming the Kingdom of God is at hand,[306] or the Blues Brothers, are on a mission from God. Unfortunately, in

this pastor's zeal to do all the right things as quickly as possible, they fall into the trap in which they "mistakenly assume that their special interests are the only things that matter"[307] and into a pattern that is arrogant, goal-driven, and hard-driving, because they are convinced that they have the best ideas. Often due to immaturity and lack of experience, they have a lack of emotional intelligence, believing that the ends justify the means. All too often the thing that overtakes their zeal for the gospel is personal ambition, which drives them to harm relationships, push congregations to change too quickly, and develop a reputation of a mover and shaker whose path is littered with human casualties.

C. S. Lewis describes prudence as a cardinal virtue defined as "practical common sense, taking the trouble to think out what you are doing and what is likely to come of it."[308] Unfortunately, with the speed with which new pastors are often expected to provide solutions to struggling congregations, the common sense approach Lewis spoke of is no longer common, and not only abandons the virtue of prudence, but its kissing cousin virtue, patience.[309] Too often leaders, once a problem has been identified, are driven to find the most expedient solution they can find and apply it, even before fully vetting its merits, especially if their ambitious drive wants a quick win. This is similar to the biblical accounts of the children of Israel, who impatiently pressed forward with their plans because they satisfied short-term desires, though the long-term outcome inevitably resulted in negative consequences. This was illustrated when Moses went to the mountain to meet with God and the people "...forgot His works,"[310] falling into idol worship in the desert as they became impatient for Moses to return, as well as through Israel's insistence on having a king to rule over them, which resulted in the tumultuous reign of King Saul.[311]

▲ ▲ ▲

Too Much, Too Fast

A modern-day example of this occurred during the first months of a newly-hired pastor's service at a church that had gone through a difficult period of decline due to the previous long-time pastor's poor health and inability to make programmatic and stylistic changes to the methods and practices of the church in order to remain relevant to the culture of the community which they served. The new pastor was eager to put the church on a new trajectory and zealous about initiating many changes in the ways the church functioned. While it was agreed upon by most in the congregation, the church leadership, and the staff that it was imperative to evaluate and begin the process of re-inventing virtually every ministry in the church, the new pastor failed to practice due diligence in regard to the culture, heritage, and aspirations of his new church. Proverbs instructs, "Know well the condition of your flocks and give attention to your herds,"[312] but the new pastor ignored this, proceeding with a series of radical changes before fully assessing the situation.

Because of the pastor's lack of prudence and patience, what could have been a period of celebration and positive foresight became stress- and tension-filled as he entered the scene with guns drawn, shooting at anything he perceived to be in his way. This resulted in people pushing back against what some felt was too much change forced upon them too quickly without their input or any regard for how it affected their church experience. The need for change was not disputed; however, the zeal, disregard for those who had remained faithful through the difficulties, and impatience in which changes were implemented created an unnecessarily adversarial environment, which resulted in the casualties of damaged relationships, eroded trust, and loss of goodwill. The pastor would often tout that in his style of leadership "the best idea wins," however, he believed that he always had the best idea. Only time will tell how this pastor and this church survive their relationship. Most likely, they will both survive it and walk together into a positive future; however, not without a painful beginning.

▲ ▲ ▲

In writing to the Colossians, Paul writes, "Put on then, as God's chosen ones, holy and beloved, compassionate hearts, kindness, humility, meekness, and patience."[313] Each of these qualities could certainly be applied to how the zealous pastor described above should have handled things better; however, if the new pastor had merely slowed down his pace of change and insistence that only he had the best ideas, many of the negative results could have been avoided, including his own heartache and frustration with those who pushed back against his initiatives. A simple way this could have been accomplished would have been to follow Proverbs' instruction to seek "many advisors"[314] and be willing to "listen to advice and accept instruction."[315] Merely going through the patient process of being open would have helped others to feel that they had a voice in the affairs of their church and buy into a future vision that was undeniably going to be beneficial for the long-term health of the church they loved.

The challenge for the 21st century lay leader, then, is to help your well-meaning, but zealous, pastor recognize the value of virtuous patience. This may not be easy in a culture that has become addicted to leadership by 15-second videos, instant messaging, and 140 characters; however, while speed is often viewed as the currency of modern business,[316] it can have disastrous consequences that affect an organization's most valuable asset, people,[317] particularly in churches.[318] Lay leaders may easily be drawn to a zealous leader who promises to deliver a complete church turn-around in record time, but buyer beware! You want to avoid the casualties of a zealous leader who lacks humble intelligence.

▲ ▲ ▲

> When the humility factor is added to the leadership style of **Zealot**, the humble pastor outcome is that brokenness, openness, and self-awareness will help this leader to be more genuinely collaborative and empathetic. They will slow down their pace and gain patience as they drive to succeed. It may be difficult for the leader to do so, and people may still grow weary of the constant push, but with effort and patience from both leader and follower, a balance can be reached.

▲ ▲ ▲

Segue: An Inspiring Story

Congratulations! You have made it through a crash course in leadership theory, but by doing so, I hope you have a better understanding of the kind of pastor you are looking to hire, or the one you already have. Before we continue discussing how the humility factor transforms leadership styles for the better, let's take a moment to catch our breath. Let me share some excerpts from the story of a pastor who exhibits humble intelligence, as reported by columnist J. Lee Grady.

Six Hour Commute...Walking

> In Malawi, one of the poorest countries in the world, Christians suffer from a severe lack of resources, but

that doesn't stop them from sharing their faith or planting churches. In fact, their wholehearted sacrifice puts America's well-funded evangelistic efforts to shame. Pastor Donald Kuyokwa is a 60-year-old Pentecostal Holiness pastor who has done more on his shoestring budget than some American denominations do with their generous donations.

A retired teacher, Kuyokwa and his wife live on a $200 monthly pension. They raised their eight children in a three-bedroom house with a corrugated iron roof and concrete floors. Their toilet is outside. Kuyokwa's small congregation in the village of Misuku collects an average of 600 kwacha every week. That comes to about 83 cents. Yet the pastor has planted four branch churches in the past sixteen years, relying mostly on the strength of his legs to walk long distances. A few years ago the lanky pastor decided to target the village of Chikando, which is located in northern Malawi near the border of Zambia. There are no roads to Chikando, only a rocky path through a dense forest. It takes Kuyokwa six hours to make the hike.

No one in Chikando had heard of Jesus when he visited the first time, but slowly people began to convert to Jesus as a result of the pastor's visits. Today the congregation has built a church with a grass roof. They use kerosene lamps during worship services because Chikando, like most of Malawi, doesn't have electricity. Pastor Kuyokwa walks to Chikando twice a month. In the past he rode a motorcycle, but it fell into disrepair. He can't ride a bicycle because the footpath has too many steep hills. So he buys cheap tennis shoes until they wear out, then he buys another pair.

Kuyokwa says he gets his inspiration from the apostle Paul in the Bible. "Paul went to places where no one had taken the gospel," he says. "Evangelists don't visit my area. They only go to the big cities." Kuyokwa is known for his bright smile. Supernatural joy obviously sustains him. He's one of the poorest people around, and he has never known suburban comforts such as air conditioning, indoor plumbing, hot showers or television. He doesn't even own a car. But when I asked him what makes him happy, Kuyokwa didn't even pause to answer. He smiled again and said, "I'm looking beyond this life. I want to meet Jesus. That's what keeps me encouraged."

We should all do some serious soul searching after hearing of this humble hero.[319]

⚊ ⚊ ⚊

Let's Review

In the last two chapters, we have thoroughly described each of the seven signs in the humility factor and looked at the many leadership styles which most pastors represent. You will recall the original formula: Humble intelligence is the result of the presence of all the humility factor actions, and when humble intelligence is added to any leadership style, it improves it because the leader leads more like Jesus led. They become a humble pastor.

$$\text{Sum of HF} = \text{HI} \; + \; L \; = \; HP$$

It should be noted that people don't begin life as humble; they usually start out from the opposite perspective. Humility is a learned behavior developed through applying the seven attributes of compassion, sacrificial service, openness, brokenness, self-awareness, forgiveness, and gratitude. One may be a fantastic natural and developed leader, or one may have the attributes of being humble; however, where the magic happens is when the two come together.

Take a look at the table below and see again that when humble intelligence is added to any leadership style, every style improves, better equipping your current or next pastor to serve your congregation.

Application of Humble Intelligence to Leadership Styles

Leadership Style Dominant Traits	Plus HI Equals HP Outcome
Authentic Leader has self-awareness, clear moral perspective, discipline, relational transparency and purpose-driven focus.	Leader draws people to themselves and their cause. Positive qualities are amplified, while negative qualities fall aside due to heightened self-awareness and a broken and meek spirit.
Autocratic-Command-and-Control Leader has positional power: "Do it because I said so." They are inflexible, intimidating, unwilling to listen to others' views, impatient, and consider questioning directives to be disloyal.	Leader becomes a strong, effective leader balanced by gentleness and compassion and open to the ideas and opinions of others.
Charismatic Leader has the ability to inspire, motivate, or coerce people to action; excellent communication skills; a bigger-than-life personality; and charm.	Leader inspires others and keeps their talent for influencing others under control through sacrificial service to others.
Coaching Leader is able to help others find solutions, asks	Leader continually learns from their interaction with those

great questions, and is a great listener. | they coach. They become better leaders as they see qualities in others which need to be addressed in themselves.

Cross-Cultural Leader has an understanding of various cultures and is tolerant, open, accepting, and agile. | Leader has a greater ability to see cultures and individuals through a lens of acceptance, understanding, and compassion.

Democratic-Participative Leader uses a safe environment to make group decisions through discussion. They have excellent listening and delegation skills, a team orientation, and a belief that everyone is valuable. | Leader becomes a collaborative leader with a high level of emotional intelligence and healthy, open relationships among team members. They model forgiveness, gratitude, compassion, and service.

Foresight Leader is future-thinking, innovative, open, entrepreneurial, and an opportunist. | The all-about-the-future leader becomes grounded in the present through the development of relational mastery.

Humble Leader is collaborative, thinks higher of others than themselves, shares decisions and authority, gives away credit, and is self-aware. | Leader becomes a better version of themselves and, due to their broken spirit, resists the tendency to become proud of their humility.

Laissez-Faire Leader uses delegation and hands-off supervision, thus appearing dispassionate.

While keeping their laid-back approach to management, this leader becomes highly relational and quietly serves others on the team.

Narcissistic Leader is extremely self-focused and feels entitled, thus feeling threatened by others' success. They reward those who benefit them, have difficulty sharing, are generous only when it makes them look good, and have situational ethics.

Perhaps the most difficult of the styles to be affected by humble intelligence, the leader, through awareness and brokenness, begins the difficult journey to learn to think of others before they naturally and habitually think of themselves. This will also be greatly helped by the leader's intentionally and anonymously serving others.

Pacesetting Leader gives high energy to achieving, moving so fast it is difficult for others to keep up, and is highly critical of those who aren't as driven to succeed. They have unreasonable expectations of employees.

Self-awareness and openness will alert this leader to their tendency to push too hard and expect too much, hopefully before their followers quit. However, it may take losing good people in order to bring about a brokenness that will lead to a less-driving manner of leadership.

Pharisee Leader is legalistic, arrogant, uncaring, and relationally deficient. They are egotists who believe the ends justify the means and that they are the only ones to whom God speaks, thus they deserve to make and enforce the rules and to be held in honor.	The most important aspects of humble intelligence for this leader will be the development of compassion, forgiveness, and openness. Once in place, they will be able to continue to uphold high standards, but do so with a softer, loving touch.
Resonant Leader has emotional intelligence: self-awareness, empathy, self-management, social awareness, and relational management.	All qualities will be enhanced as the leader increases their service to others with an emerging broken spirit.
Selfless Leader sacrifices for the benefit of others, gives the spotlight to others, and is always encouraging.	Qualities of compassion, gratitude, and forgiveness will emerge through the leader's growing awareness of brokenness.
Servant Leader desires to serve others and puts others' needs ahead of their own. They are sacrificial, relational, and empathetic.	Heightened self-awareness and brokenness will complete the package of a leader who considers others' needs before their own.

Shepherd Leader is highly relational and prefers to spend the majority of their time with the people they serve rather than doing administrative tasks. They are caring and empathetic and are good counselors who will help others through their challenges and make them feel loved. When necessary, they will correct the behavior of a member of the flock by swatting them with their shepherd's staff.	Every quality of humble intelligence will be enhanced in the shepherd leader, benefiting both the shepherd and the members of their flock.
Situational Leader is agile, analytical, a strong decision-maker, and open.	The softer skills related to relationships will make this decisive leader more approachable.
Strategic Leader is a long-term thinker, analytical, decisive, and action- and results-oriented.	Similar to situational leaders, the softer skills will make the relational aspect of leading a team better for everyone.
Transactional Leader is goal- and rewards-oriented and results-driven within a reciprocal relational context. They have good negotiation skills.	Self-awareness and brokenness will provide the leader a gentler approach to achievement.

Transformational Leader has the ability to convince others to be a part of organizational change and inspire them to a higher level of commitment, empowering them to do the work through their motivational words.

Brokenness and compassion will help this leader to keep their ego in check as they become successful and effective.

Visionary Leader is people-oriented, creative, and goal-oriented. They are dreamers with the ability to transform ideas into reality.

Similarly to transformational leaders, brokenness and self-awareness will remind this successful leader that life is not merely about them and what they can achieve.

Zealot Leader is arrogant, goal-driven, and convinced they have the best ideas. They have a lack of emotional intelligence and believe that the ends justify the means.

Brokenness, openness, and self-awareness will help this leader to be more genuinely collaborative and empathetic. They will slow down their pace and gain patience as they drive to succeed.

▲ ▲ ▲

Finally, you will also remember how, once someone has developed humble intelligence and it is influencing their leadership style, they will be continually strengthened as the process moves forward. The more humble intelligence, the more leadership qualities are strengthened, which leads to an even greater depth of the humility factor, leading to more humble intelligence, and so on. The point is that once someone is practicing the signs of the humility factor, they continue to grow in their humble intelligence, greatly benefiting the church.

In chapter five, we will discuss the process of using the humility factor when hiring your next pastor, and I will include an assessment tool for you to use. You are ready to put all you've learned into practice!

Healthy churches are led by humble pastors.

CHAPTER 5

It's Time to Hire a New Pastor!

How to Hire a Pastor with the Humility Factor in Mind

Churches are what are referred to as living systems, in which all parts are interdependent upon each other. Take one away, and the system as a whole will become unhealthy and may even cease to exist. 2 Corinthians discusses this in the context of the body of Christ needing all of the parts which come together for the good of the whole.[320] Pastor Douglas Hall describes churches in this manner through his metaphor entitled *The Cat and the Toaster*.[321] Both the cat and the toaster are comprised of many parts that are needed for the whole to function properly, but what makes the cat a living system and the toaster not is that the toaster can be taken apart and put back together again, however, if you try to take the cat apart and then reassemble it, you will not only kill the cat, but put yourself in harm's way as you try! Churches, like the cat, need all of their parts, so if you try to remove one, you jeopardize the church as a whole. Since living systems are non-linear and more of a matrix, they cannot be directed without the understanding that unforeseen consequences are inevitable. However, with the right person at the helm, the system can be disturbed in such a way as to encourage progress toward a desired outcome.[322]

This is why choosing the right pastor is so important. They will be a key component in both the health of a church and the achievement of a desired outcome, providing that they have both the leadership skills required and also the signs of the humility factor. One lay leader quoted in *Christian Century* magazine who was hiring their new lead pastor said, "It's sad that we can't be too careful about whom we choose. We must know just about everything there is to know about the person we call."[323] My advice to him is to heed the words of God recorded by the prophet Isaiah, "This is the one to whom I will look: he who is humble and contrite in spirit and trembles at my word,"[324] and begin by looking for evidence of the humility factor. Also, remember that when it comes to hiring, "one size does not fit all."[325] There are specific things to look for which are universal to all churches, but also some which are specific to a particular church with unique needs. We will discuss those in a moment.

Bad Hires

It is important that when hiring a new lead pastor, church lay leaders get it right, because the costs of removing a bad hire are high in actual dollars as well as in time, emotion, energy, congregational trust, and general goodwill. Hiring a new pastor must be done with great due diligence and special care. The author of the book *Humble and Strong* warns that tremendous damage can be done by a bad leader, and with time, it is gradually harder and harder to repair. A bad hire will weaken a church, causing it to become less resilient than it used to be, and it may end up existing in a persistent vegetative state.[326] I believe it is safe to assume that being in such a state is not what churches desire, so getting it right is critical. Holly Tate, of the church leadership placement organization Vanderbloemen, spoke of the need for churches to have a "bad hire fund in order to mitigate some of the costs associated with the transition of a staff member who was a poor fit."[327] The company even includes a "bad hire calculator" on their website, so obviously this is not an uncommon occurrence. Lay leaders must invest the time and energy to find the person who will be the exact fit they need. Rushing through so that everyone can pat themselves on the back and get back to real life begs for conflict and strife, and creates the need for even more time to be invested later. Search committees must sweat the small stuff because they are always a bigger deal than they appear at first.[328]

What to Look For

Chapter three described in detail the attributes of the humility factor, which I believe must be part of the hiring process if you want a pastor with humble intelligence who will lead your church to a healthy state. Chapter four gave you a broad overview of the many leadership styles from which you may choose for your next pastor, depending on your unique circumstances. Later in this chapter, I provide an assessment tool for you to use in this process. In addition, let's take a look at some of the other general qualifications to look for that apply to virtually all of the pastoral candidates you will encounter.

Let's begin with the underlying theme of this book and a statement from Pastor Standish, who transformed my understanding of what it means to be a great and humble leader. He says, "Humility, in the end, is a state of being in which we willingly try to seek and serve God's will in everything."[329] This is echoed by Sanders in *Spiritual Leadership* when he states, "Humility is a hallmark of the spiritual leader."[330] From my viewpoint, these two authors state the obvious starting point when considering who to hire as the next lead pastor of a church. While the candidates may have a host of talents, experience, and education, at the foundation of who they are should be humility, which includes the seven attributes described in chapter three. As a lay leader, you will want to know for certain that God's blessing will be upon the person you place in the lead position. Scripture states, "He leads the humble in what is right, and teaches the humble his way."[331] This assurance that your pastor is being led in the right direction and is following the ways of God will help your church to be healthy and you to sleep at night.

Raw Materials

Most church leaders will agree, and scripture supports, that in the hiring process, there must be an emphasis on character and living a life that is above reproach.[332] They may have made some mistakes in their decisions in the past, but they used these instances as times to grow.[333] Next, look for evidence that they have an internal drive and desire to answer the call to your church and ministry. Their work ethic must be stellar, because, as we all know, church ministry is not for the faint of heart. Contrary to what many congregation members may believe about the work life of a pastor, it is extremely demanding and hard work, and immersed in emotional intensity. Your potential pastor must also accept and embrace the rollercoaster of joys and challenges experienced when working with church people.

The final raw material is talent and giftedness. Leaders must be foundationally equipped by God for the work to which He has called them. While 1 Corinthians 12 outlines many gifts given to believers by God for His service and demonstrates that none is more important than another, there is the implication that gifts are specifically and not generally given. Not everyone is a singer or a preacher. Some, rather, are gifted with other behind-the-scenes abilities which are less observable, but just as important. It is necessary for your future leader to embrace the call and the gift of God uniquely designed for them, and for your church to accept the same. I would recommend that prior to putting out the call for resumes, you compose a clear and comprehensive list of qualities that you believe your church needs. Avoid using a generic pastoral template, as no two churches are exactly alike. It will take some effort, but it is effort well spent. All in all, when evaluating who might become your next pastor, it should be remembered that "identity is the culmination of one's values, experiences, and self-perceptions,"[334] all of which can be found in the raw materials.

Shared Values and Vision

One of the things that was to Joshua's advantage when succeeding Moses was that they were perfectly aligned with each other in the vision of what God was doing for the children of Israel. There was no conflict as to what was important, who was ultimately in charge, and why they were doing what they were doing. Joshua and Moses had shared values and vision that allowed for a seamless succession from one leader to the next. According to Dess and Picken, "Effectively employed, a [shared] strategic vision provides a clear future direction; a framework for the organization's mission and goals; and enhanced communication, participation, and commitment."[335] One of the critical things to look for in your next pastor is the congruence of values and vision for a shared future between your church and them. Even though it is inevitable that changes will be made in methods along the way, there should be an immediate alignment of values and ultimate mission.

Anointing

It is important for pastors to be called of God, which theological scholars identify as the "biblical charismatic imperative," ensuring leaders are called and anointed by God.[336] If this is not the case, potential leaders may flame out under the physical, emotional, or spiritual pressures of ministry. All too often good people become casualties of church work simply because they may have tried to force or manufacture their calling and be something they were never intended to be. Moses had the luxury of knowing for certain that Joshua was anointed because God told him so, but Elijah was not as certain with Elisha. In David's story, God said, "I have found in David the son of Jesse a man after my own heart, who will do all my will,"[337] and in Solomon's, God said, "It is Solomon your son who shall build my house and my courts, for I have chosen him to be my son, and I will be his father,"[338] so anointing was never in question. You must look for and be certain that if the person you are considering hiring is to be your next pastor, they are anointed by God to be so.

Humility Toward God

We dealt with this subject in both the first chapter as part of the introduction and when discussing self-awareness in the humility factor attributes in chapter three, so this is somewhat of a review. However, the importance of having a true understanding of who we are in comparison to God cannot be overstated. The apostle Paul writes, "For the wisdom of this world is folly with God,"[339] meaning that it really doesn't matter how talented, educated, or intelligent someone is, they do not hold a candle to God! As said before, it is crucial that our pastors get this. They must lead with humility, understanding that though they have been granted positional power, they are to function as a "first among equals"[340] in regard to the other pastors and allow God to be in final control of their church. They are to do as the great kings of Israel did, have a humble dependence on God[341] and be radically open to God's guidance.[342] The modern church desperately needs leaders who will subjugate their agenda to God with the understanding that glory, honor, praise, and credit belong to Him and Him alone. Note that when the book of Revelation states, "Worthy are you, our Lord and God, to receive glory and honor and power, for you created all things, and by your will they existed and were created," it doesn't make any mention of God needing anyone's help—not a church board, not a committee, and not a pastor! It must be the other way around. He's God; we're not. He doesn't need our help, but we need His!

But We Already Have a Pastor!

At this point, you may be thinking about the pastor that you currently have leading your church. They may or may not exhibit signs of humble intelligence. If they don't, all is not lost. However, attaining it will take their willingness to change and grow into the humble pastor described in this book, and it will take a great amount of patience by church leaders to allow the pastor the time they need to grow. I would advise asking a pastoral coach to come alongside your pastor in order to facilitate the learning process. There may be someone in your church right now who is qualified and whom the pastor trusts, or you may want to use a professional counselor or someone who specializes in this type of coaching on a pastor-to-pastor level.

Assessing if Your Candidate Shows Signs of the Humility Factor

The following is a compilation and modification of the questions which were included at the end of each description of the seven signs of the humility factor, plus a ranking system in which you will give a numeric rating (0-4 with 4 being highest) for each question. If the pastoral candidate shows no evidence of the humility factor attribute, score a zero, and if they exhibit convincing evidence of the attribute, score a four. Once all the questions have been answered, add up the total. Keep in mind that this is a subjective assessment and you should use discernment in order to answer the questions. Allow the Holy Spirit to guide you as you consider each candidate. The final total is not a scientifically-controlled answer and should not be the only data considered when choosing a pastor, but it does provide valuable perspective as to if the potential pastor will be a humble leader or not.

Healthy churches are led by humble pastors.

The Humility Factor Assessment Instrument

Please note that this is a subjective assessment and discernment by the interviewer is encouraged.

Compassion

1. How well does the pastoral candidate show signs of empathy by being genuinely interested in and caring about the people they serve? (0-4)_____
2. How well do they appear to listen? (0-4)_____
3. How well do they exhibit grace when dealing with people who have made poor choices? (0-4)_____
4. How well do they appear to be willing to walk alongside someone to restore them to ministry and fellowship? (0-4)_____
5. How well do they appear to follow Jesus' command to "love thy neighbor"? (0-4)_____
6. How well do they appear to show love and care to others in practical ways without bias or preference? (0-4)_____

Sacrificial Service

1. Does the pastoral candidate appear to be willing to put their own needs aside in order to meet the needs of others? (0-4)_____
2. Do they appear unmotivated by recognition and rewards for their service? (0-4)_____
3. Do they appear to be willing to do whatever needs to get done without feeling that some things are below them? (0-4)_____

DR. JOHN PLASTOW

Openness

1. In the pastoral candidate, is there evidence of being a lifelong learner? (0-4) _____
2. Do they appear to seek and value the input of other people? (0-4) _____
3. To what extent do they appear to take the time to listen to the leading of the Holy Spirit through prayer and consideration without pushing their own agenda? (0-4) _____

Brokenness

1. To what extent would you expect the pastoral candidate to willingly collaborate with others? (0-4) _____
2. Is there evidence that they will submit to the higher authority of God and the governing board? (0-4) _____
3. Though strong in abilities, how much evidence is there of a gentle and meek underlying spirit? (0-4) _____

Self-Awareness

1. To what extent does the pastoral candidate understand where he stands in comparison to God? (0-4) _____
2. To what extent do they appear to downplay the adulation of their congregation? (0-4) _____

3. To what extent do they have an authentic view of their strengths and weaknesses? (0-4)_____
4. To what extent do they appear to be honest with themselves? (0-4)_____

Forgiveness

1. Does the pastoral candidate appear to have put aside bitterness toward any person, group, or their previous church? (0-4)_____
2. Do they appear to pass along the same level of forgiveness which has been given to them? (0-4)_____
3. Is there evidence that they reconcile broken relationships when they occur? (0-4)_____

Gratitude

1. Does the pastoral candidate appear grateful for what is provided by God and the church? (0-4)_____
2. Do they appear to have a humble attitude towards material rewards and places of honor? (0-4)_____
3. Is there evidence that when circumstances are tough, they acknowledge the blessings of God? (0-4)_____

Total Score _____

100	Perfectly demonstrates evidence of the humility factor and humble intelligence
90-99	Much evidence of the humility factor and will soon grow into humble intelligence
80-89	Well on the way, but some effort is needed to achieve humble intelligence
70-79	Needs a lot of effort and attention, but there is hope
60-69	Without a major change of heart, will not achieve humble intelligence
59-Below	Will require God's intervention in order to be open to the humility factor

Copies of the Humility Factor Assessment Instrument are available for free download at www.humblepastors.org. Please note that this assessment tool will be tested over time. Please provide me your feedback at the website.

CHAPTER 6
Humility Matters

So What? Who Cares? What's at Stake?

As I was casting the research net through interviews, surveys, and Google searches, I had many tell me of pastors whom they considered to be humble. One of these is Andy Stanley, the senior pastor of North Point Community Church in Atlanta, GA. His work as a pastor, speaker, and author is highly heralded and his church gives every indication that it is healthy. Here is an excerpt from one of his messages given at the Catalyst conference in 2006.

"Reek with Humility"

> The Most High is sovereign over the kingdoms of men, and he gives them to whoever he wishes. Leadership is stewardship. It is temporary and can be taken away; we are always accountable. God puts people in leadership. People love to follow humble leaders. There is a self-centeredness involved in leadership that is inherent—the question is how do we deal with this? We deal with this by waking up every morning and saying, "The Most High is

sovereign over the kingdoms of men and he gives them to whoever he wishes." Many of us have worked with leaders that get arrogant, that started out great and that are Christians, but they get so arrogant and it hurts them. Men and women get caught up in their own press releases.

Of all the leaders in the world, our hallmark should be humility—we should reek with humility because we wake up every morning and realize that God put us in the place that we are in. You are where you are because in some sovereign way God placed you where you are and he can take this away any time—this should liberate you and allow you to lead fearlessly. John the Baptist, Jesus, King David; these leaders stepped out of the way because they knew God was in control. Lead with all your heart, without fear, and with humility.[343]

▲ ▲ ▲

Stanley obviously understands from a pastoral standpoint what even businesses in the marketplace are beginning to grasp. "Humility is essential,"[344] states corporate consultant William McKnight, and the relevance of humility is increasing in conversations regarding the globalization of organizations that are rapidly becoming more complex and diverse as they expand their boundaries.[345] Still, even though humility is gaining its own "street cred," it is often still a less-admired skill in political and business circles.[346] It is my primary premise that healthy churches are led by humble pastors, but I also believe that the humility factor can and should be applied to secular industry as well. Healthy companies, I believe, when described as those who take good care of their people, offer a good value to their customers, and are good citizens of their local and global communities, are also led by humble leaders.

Honestly, though, who really cares? As long as a product is a good value, should I care if the leader is humble? In relation to the marketplace, that is a question for another book, but you've already figured out my answer as it applies to churches and pastors. A church can have every program one can imagine, terrific services, a fantastic children's ministry and all the bells and whistles of a "successful church," but if it has an arrogant spirit due to an egocentric pastor, I believe it misses the mark of what Jesus wants us to be. In the book *Teams that Thrive*, the authors state it well,

> God's way of leading his people is through a profound humility. I see that as a model for how we should lead with humility – that intentional recognition that God is everything to you, and that you are nothing without him. Humility is the acknowledgement that life is not about you, and that the needs of others are more important than your own. Humility is an attitude, a way of thinking that touches your approach to everything you do and especially the people you come in contact with. It reminds us of Jesus, our example who humbled himself in order to serve the purposes of God and to serve us.[347]

The church must be viewed as being different than other organizations in the community. People need to know that when they call the church office, they won't be treated as merely a number, as if they had called the DMV, or strictly as a revenue source, as if they had called an electronics superstore. There must be a difference, frankly, because of what is at stake. As we discussed earlier in this book, people's eternal lives lie in the balance, so it is our responsibility to make sure that we act as Jesus acted when dealing with people who have yet to discover a relationship with the loving Savior. As Kimball states, "Christians are known as scary, angry, and judgmental,"[348] to which Bickel and Jantz add "hypercritical" and "intolerant," causing people on a spiritual quest to "avoid God simply because so many Christians are repulsive."[349] The answer is humility. Pastors with humble intelligence display the attributes of the humility factor in such a way that it attracts people to Jesus, rather than repels them. Even 75 years ago, when the relationship of the church and community was a bit friendlier, C. S. Lewis warned that to bring outsiders into the fold, churches must make sure not to show their divisions to the community. He reminded pastors that there was nothing positive about being "pig-headed" or doing the right things with the wrong attitude. Humility is the key.

How the Seven Signs Impacted Me
Earlier I told you the story of my journey to humility. Here is a little more about how the seven signs have impacted my life, which will make sense now that you understand them. From the standpoint of the seven signs of the humility factor, I have made good progress, though I hesitate to call myself humble. I still have much work to do, but I know that I am a different follower of Christ than I once was.

- My level of compassion has completely changed, as I no longer believe I have all the answers to my and everyone else's problems. Long ago, I was not overly empathetic when others were dealing with issues, particularly when I felt they had caused them. I always had the answer, which was incredibly arrogant on my part. Today I am quick to give grace and to love others without condition. I believe it is God's job to deal with people and their choices, and it is my job to just love them.
- Sacrificial service is more than a concept to be taught these days, as I have learned that I must not expect rewards from

what I do. If there is a need that I can fill, it is my responsibility to answer God's call, be it a late-night hospital call or an urgent need for counseling when I have other things that need doing. I believe all believers should be serving in some capacity, led by their pastor, who must model the way.
- Openness is definitely an improved area for me as I have become open to learning, other people, and especially the Holy Spirit. For years I thought I knew it all, and no one could tell me differently. How very foolish that was. I am glad to be free of the stress and responsibility of knowing everything now.
- Brokenness is huge for me. As I pointed out in my story, there have been many points at which I was broken only to recover and return to my old patterns, but the point at which God really first broke me was when I had to submit my will to what God wanted for me in my marriage (That's another book right there!). Then I experienced further brokenness and submission to God when I lost two professional positions which I loved and had done well, and after a nationwide search, didn't find a new position. Today I am a broken vessel, but a renewed servant of Christ.
- Self-awareness is a cornerstone of a person with humble intelligence. I am gaining valuable ground in that area. It has helped that I am a self-assessment junkie. The more I discover about myself, the more I understand my relationship to and with God.
- Forgiveness is one of the most difficult signs for me to master. I remain deeply hurt by some people whom I thought I had served well, but God has been very clear that I must forgive, even when things still sting. I am working on that and slowly making progress. The biggest change is that I want to forgive.

- <u>Gratitude</u> is another difficult thing for me, as I am a visionary who can always see how things could be better, which causes me to forget to look at all the good things that are around me. My wife is often frustrated with me because I am seldom content. Again, I am working on that. As I look to the future, I am grateful that I still have the chance to become who God created me to be.

Did We Miss Anything?

Innovation scholar and author Scott Berkun writes, "You can't find something new if you limit your travels to places others have already found."[350] This is why the focus of this book has been strictly on the discussion of the seven signs of the humility factor and why it is important for your next pastor to display humble intelligence. There are certainly many other things one should consider when wading through the stacks of resumes you will receive after you've posted your job opening, such as:

- The scriptural standards outlined specifically in 1 Timothy 3 must also be considered. These are commonly part of most pastoral searches and we discussed them earlier in the book.
- Fruit of the Spirit – What about it? It's good, too, but there is already a book written about it (The Bible!) and there are currently 5,966 books for sale on Amazon dealing with it. I suggest you add it to your process, but you don't have to read all the books available! Please note: Like the seven signs of the humility factor, the person who displays the fruit of the Spirit displays all of them, not just the ones that are convenient or easy.
- Spiritual Gifts Tests and Personality Assessments – These are certainly good to use as well. There are many assessments

available to you. I personally believe that in addition to discovering the dominant spiritual gifts of your potential pastor, you should find out more about their personality and strengths. My suggestions include the Myers-Briggs Personality Inventory, the DISC Personality Test, Emotional Intelligence Competencies, and StrengthsFinder. All of these plus many more are available online.

Of course, there is much more to hiring that could be included here. If you browse through your local bookstore or go online, there are thousands upon thousands of books that claim to have the perfect method to finding the perfect employee. However, as the quote above advises you, find the path that hasn't been used by everyone else before you. Honestly, while I would love to have many churches adopt the humility factor way of hiring their next pastor, for now, it's new. Go ahead and use it!

7 Ways How **Not** to be a Pastor of Humble Intelligence

Because there haven't been enough examples in this book (wink) of how to show humble intelligence, here are additional stories of humility in action, or in a few cases, the lack of humility. In this chapter, we will use the seven signs, but from the opposite view. In order to not be humbly intelligent, there must be a lack of each of the seven signs of the humility factor.

Lack of Compassion

How often do all of us see someone asking for food or money and we try to avoid eye contact and hurry by in order to go along with our plans? While we cannot help everyone with whom we come in contact, there should be some for whom we offer compassion.

When you are interviewing prospective pastors, see if they include stories of compassion, like the one told here.

Burrito Under the Pier (First told in my blog in 2016)

Let me tell you a true story, one that I personally experienced. My wife and I were out to dinner with a young couple. We were at a wonderful Mexican restaurant overlooking the beach in southern California. We talked for hours while we tried a variety of salsas, from mild to nuclear heat levels, and enjoyed not only each other's company, but a great meal. Soon after we were served our entrees, I noticed that the young man with us sliced his extra large burrito in two, eating only one half and wrapping up the second. I figured it was his way of stretching his food budget and that he would enjoy it the next day. I thought no more of it until later when we decided to take an after-dinner walk on the beach right next to the pier.

Before too long I noticed that our guest was looking around as if he was looking for something in particular, which I soon realized was exactly the case. Sitting up against one of the pilings under the pier was a member of the beach's homeless community, and my guest was on his way to speak with him and give him the second half of his dinner. Awesome, I thought; what a great thing to do. His girlfriend then proceeded to tell us that he does this all the time and that she never gets to take leftovers home! It turns out that he had split his burrito at dinner specifically for this purpose. He had a sincere desire to help those who have less than he, and this was his personal mission field. Again, awesome. What a wonderful example!

I tell you this story for two reasons. One is obvious – we should all show compassion and be willing to share what we have with those who are less fortunate than we are. The person under the pier was hungry, we were not; we had the rest of a huge burrito, and they didn't. It doesn't take much to figure out that the compassionate thing to do was to share. The second point is that this was an excellent example of how a servant and selfless leader functions with their people. Often the leader possesses things and has privileges that their followers do not have, so it is to everyone's advantage for the leader to share their time, energy and resources to help others out. The main point is that servant and selfless leaders make it a priority to put the needs of others above their own. They don't have to think about whether or not they are going to help others, they do it automatically. It is part of their DNA. If someone on their team has a need, they immediately jump into action trying to meet that need, be it emotional, relational, financial, spiritual or otherwise. Servant and selfless leaders do just as our friend from the beach did, plan ahead to make sure they can help others and share what they have.[351]

Note: The couple in the story is my daughter and her then-boyfriend. I must say that I have a great and humble son-in-law!

▲ ▲ ▲

Pastors without humble intelligence show a lack of compassion.

Lack of Sacrificial Service

One of the warning signs that someone lacks the humility factor attribute of sacrificial service is that they sabotage others' ministry by making it all about them. I have a friend who is a retired long-term worship pastor with whom I partnered on many large events.

All About Him (the pastor, that is)

A worship pastor friend of mine and his team did a highly successful Christmas event each year, yet he was often frustrated with his senior pastor's actions in the performances. The large cast and crew had spent months preparing a complex and highly-focused program designed to convey a specific message and lead into a "brief" wrap-up and invitation to meet Jesus by the pastor. However, even after years of working together, my friend was never sure of what to expect from his pastor, because regardless of how excellent the program was or how effectively the set-up to the invitation had been presented by the cast, the pastor would make the wrap-up all about himself, trying to get laughs and taking all of the focus for himself instead of putting it on Christ. It was insensitive and displayed clearly that the pastor was not willing to sacrificially serve in the role requested of him. Eventually my friend left for another church and the pastor remained. It's too bad that the good work of my friend ended for the people of what was really a great church. They deserved better than having a pastor who made it all about himself.

▲ ▲ ▲

I always felt so badly for my friend because, in contrast, my pastor of 18 years had always been very aware of the requirements of his part in a similar event. He felt a great responsibility to the hundreds of volunteers who had given months of their time to only use the time allotted. In fact, he would have me time him, and if he went over the limit, he would adjust. He showed that the program was not about him and he served sacrificially even when I had him show up for eleven performances plus rehearsals!

Pastors without humble intelligence show a lack of sacrificial service.

Lack of Openness

As we have discussed, part of showing openness is one's willingness to include others in the important activities of ministry. Openness means that a pastor doesn't insist on being a one-man show. Lack of openness means that on the pastor's report card, it would say, "Doesn't play well with others." Here is a great example told by Pastor Wayne Cordeiro, author of *Doing Church as a Team*, of how he learned the importance of being open to others on his team. Note: I've edited the story for length. To get the whole story, pick up a copy of his book! You'll see that there is no doubt that Pastor Cordeiro displays the attribute of openness.

Team Approach

> I think the first time I really saw it all come together was at one of our Christmas Eve services in 1996. We had a program filled with multimedia presentations, dance, mime, drama, a 100-voice choir and ensembles – I mean, the works! The auditorium was filled with more than 1,200 people, many who were there for the very first time. I stood just offstage, watching the evening unfold. Sometime during this program, it hit me. As I watched our outstanding keyboardist play the piano with all his heart, I thought to

myself, *He is preaching the gospel the best way he knows how – through his piano!*

Nearby, another was playing drums with his usual excellence and I thought, *He is preaching the gospel the best way he knows how – through his drums!* I looked into the radiant faces of the choir, where I saw many lives that had recently been transformed by the Lord's grace, and I said to myself, *Those wonderful people are all preaching the gospel the best way they know how – through their singing!* The mime, the drama team, dancers, and the ensemble were all preaching the gospel through their gifts. Then I noticed the stage coordinators moving with poise and rhythm, rearranging microphones and straightening cords. I saw video people running cameras. I saw ushers, too.

Then I walked out onto the platform, picked up a microphone and wrapped up the evening with a simple presentation of the gospel message. Yes, through speaking, I, too, was preaching the gospel the best way I knew how, but I wasn't doing it alone. We were all doing it together. We were preaching the gospel message the best way we knew how – through our gifts. And that included the children's workers, parking team and everyone who had worked behind the scenes to make this evening happen. Every single person had a part. This evening was not one presentation of the gospel, but several hundred presentations of the gospel – all at the same time in one evening. That's what made it so powerful! I started to see it clearly, and I was flooded with a whole new understanding of how beautiful the Body of Christ can be. We were doing church as a team.[352]

▲ ▲ ▲

> *Pastors without humble intelligence show a lack of openness.*

Lack of Brokenness
We have already devoted a lot of time to the subject of brokenness and how leaders with humble intelligence have gone through difficult periods in their lives in which their wills were broken and they ultimately submitted their lives to God's plan instead of fighting for their own. Another example is that of Joseph in Genesis. This is one of the oldest accounts we have of leaders in the Bible, but also one of the best, because Joseph was one who began life very sure of himself, to the point that his own brothers sold him into slavery. However, through a long process of taking a step forward, then getting knocked back again, Joseph eventually became the ultimate second chair leader to Pharaoh,[353] overseeing all affairs for Egypt during a severe famine, saving his family and all of Egypt from certain death. The story of Joseph outlines the many times when Joseph lost everything, but each time rebounded and discovered who he was and more importantly, who God was. Joseph, once a dreamer with the desire to gloat of his fortune to others, gradually was broken, and therefore willing to take a second chair not only to the Pharaoh, but ultimately to God. Humble pastors display the same brokenness and submission.

> *Pastors without humble intelligence show a lack of brokenness.*

Lack of Self-Awareness
The first time I heard a lead pastor say from the platform during a worship service, "I'm one of the ministers here," I was pretty impressed. I thought that it was cool that the pastor didn't set himself

up as being the only pastor that mattered at that church. Then I watched that pastor during the week and quickly realized that the humility which I thought I had observed was really false humility put on to give the appearance of team-based ministry. The next time I heard a pastor say the same thing, I was again impressed by it, but I was a little skeptical because of my last experience. Then I heard it again and again. Apparently, the words "I am one of the ministers here" was the trendy thing to say and many pastors were adopting its use. I can't count how many hundreds of times I've heard those words, and to be honest, used those words. I believe it makes a good statement about the church and its pastors, provided it is authentic and true.

I'm sure that many who say those words or similar ones mean what they say. I have heard some of whom I'm certain of their sincerity; however, I've also experienced disingenuous pastors who speak of team, but operate with a dictatorial hand. These pastors need to dive into the deep end of self-awareness so that they may discover who they are in the eyes of self and others, but mostly in the sight of God. Their false humility is, in essence, a form of deceit, which scripture states that God hates.[354] The pastors you are considering need to show evidence that they understand their place in the hierarchy of God's kingdom. No false humility allowed. If they say that they are "one of the ministers," they had better mean it.

> ***Pastors without humble intelligence***
> ***show a lack of self-awareness.***

Lack of Forgiveness

As I stated earlier in this chapter, this is the aspect of the humility factor upon which I am actively focusing. Ministry has so many times when difficult decisions must be made, feelings get hurt, and relationships become strained and even broken. Forgiveness is a big issue for many pastors, especially the longer they are in the ministry. A very sad example which I observed from a distance and can merely speculate upon is the rise and fall of the Crystal Cathedral in Southern California. As you know from my story, I worked with the church right out of college, so I have a minimal inside view, though from a long time ago. When I worked there, the Garden Grove Community Church was at its height, which is what propelled them into the grand adventure of building the cathedral and subsequent additional facilities. I must say that my memories of the environment, effectiveness, and energy of a church that was making things happen are positive.

Unfortunately, through the years difficulties arose, at least in part from internal struggles among Pastor Schuller's family. Many articles have been written about what caused the downfall of the church, including direct interviews with Robert A. Schuller, who had been groomed to take over for his dad as the senior pastor.[355] Through various articles, it becomes apparent that there were extreme power struggles between family members who wanted the opportunity to lead the church after Robert H. Schuller's retirement, leading to rifts in the family that were impossible to repair.

From my viewpoint, I see a series of actions fueled by the inability and unwillingness to forgive those who had hurt them, which caused estrangement with little hope of reconciliation. This example is within a family, but it is all too common in the family of God as well. Pastors and members, pastors and pastors, and members and members can disagree on any number of issues which explode into a fight-to-the-death scenario causing broken relationships, the dismantling of ministries, church splits, and lost opportunities to do the work God called churches to do. When this happens, the devil wins.

> *Pastors without humble intelligence show a lack of forgiveness.*

Lack of Gratitude
One of the opposites of gratitude is greed. A pastor that has the humility factor attribute of gratitude demonstrates that they are thankful for the blessings of God, the generosity of the church, and the relationships which are nurtured with the people they serve. However, greed is a tool the devil uses to take away a pastor's gratitude, and ultimately their humble intelligence. Pastors with a lack of gratitude will begin to continually ask for higher salaries, more perks, and increased time off, plus take advantage of relationships with influential people in the congregation and community. While there is nothing wrong with a pastor having a nice home and a new car, when those become status symbols for the pastor and one car becomes six parked outside the nicest home of anyone in the congregation, an issue of greed may have crept in.

This is an area that can easily become a problem for a pastor, especially when they have been around for a long time and helped the church to be highly visible, effective, and successful. Governing boards often want to reward their pastor for a job well done (and they should), but too often it goes too far and becomes a gravy train that is impossible to stop. In addition, many times the obsession to have more takes down pastors who began their ministry with the intent to serve God and people, but were seduced by greed. Joe McKeever says on The Crosswalk website,

> The war to remain humble must be fought on many fronts every day of our lives. Even then, pride will slip up on us and enter from our blind side. Before we know it, we will start sounding as though we deserve more from God and others than we are getting, like we have been mistreated

in life, as though the universe was built for our comfort and our being deprived of anything ranks as a great injustice.[356]

Earlier in the book, we discussed the downfall of Jim Bakker, but there are many examples from which to choose, including the founding pastor of Yoido Full Gospel, the largest church in Korea, who, in 2014, was convicted of embezzling $12 million of church funds.[357] As you evaluate candidates for your open position, look at their lifestyle and attitudes toward salary, benefits, and perks. Be fair and generous, but make sure that the pastor displays genuine gratitude.

> **Pastors without humble intelligence show a lack of gratitude.**

An Unparalleled Example

I've spent this entire book attempting to convince you that healthy churches are led by humble pastors. I outlined the seven signs of the humility factor, described 22 leadership styles, and demonstrated how when the two are added together, the result is a better leader who leads more like Jesus led. I've given you many examples of humble and not-so-humble pastors and true-life stories of churches that show the benefits of humble intelligence or the challenges of the lack thereof. I've even tried to give you a glimpse of my own personal journey. If you still need convincing, let me take out my final example, who is no doubt one of the greatest examples of a humble pastor the world has ever known, Billy Graham.

Proverbs states, "The reward for humility and fear of the Lord is riches and honor and life,"[358] and each of these is evident in Pastor Graham's life. Though he would never boast, he has had earthly rewards in material possessions because of his notoriety, books, and speaking. For years, he was considered "America's pastor," and made regular trips to the White House and participated in the swearing-in of presidents. Due to his extensive world travel through missions and revivals, few people in the world have the fame and honor which he has, and this year he will celebrate his 99th birthday.

The following is a short description of one person's encounter with Billy Graham.

Such an Honor

> The first time I met Billy Graham, he took my hand to shake it and said, "It is an honor to meet you." I was stunned. Here was one of the most famous men in the world, and he humbly spoke of the honor of meeting me. I could hardly refrain from saying, "I'm me. You're Graham. You've got this honor thing backwards."[359]

▲ ▲ ▲

Can you imagine Billy Graham saying that it was "an honor to meet you?" Actually, yes, because that is the kind of humble pastor he is. On the Billy Graham website, there is an article that outlines Billy's *12 Things to Humble Yourself,* written by Janet Chismar.[360] As you read this list, you will see how the seven signs of the humility factor align with it and how these form an excellent blueprint for all pastors to follow as they lead the church.

- Routinely confess your sin to God (Brokenness)
- Acknowledge your sin to others (Brokenness)
- Take wrong patiently (Compassion: Love)
- Actively submit to authority...the good and the bad (Openness)

- Receive correction and feedback from others graciously (Openness)
- Accept a lowly place (Self-Awareness)
- Purposefully associate with people of a lower state than you (Compassion: Empathy and Love)
- Choose to serve others (Sacrificial Service)
- Be quick to forgive (Forgiveness)
- Cultivate a grateful heart (Gratitude)
- Purpose to speak well of others (Self-Awareness)
- Treat pride as a condition that always necessitates embracing the cross (Brokenness)

In this book we have highlighted many great examples of humble pastors, and few would argue that Billy Graham is one of the most humble pastors of all time. Graham follows the example set by Jesus and many other faithful servants in Christian church history, including St. Augustine, who stated, "Should you ask me: What is the first thing in religion? I should reply: The first, second, and third thing therein is humility."[361]

Healthy churches are led by humble pastors.

Final Thoughts from a Work in Progress

> In the book *Love Does*, Bob Goff states,
> God loves the humble ones, and the humble ones often don't make it as first-round draft picks for the jobs with big titles or positions. But they always seem to be the first-round picks for God when he's looking for someone to use in a big way. Jesus' message is a simple one. We all get a chance to be awesome if we want to be. Not surprisingly, the way to do it best is by being secretly incredible.[362]

I must admit, as hard as I've tried sometimes, I've never achieved "first-round draft pick" status. I wish I could say that that fact didn't bother me, but sadly, it does. I've always struggled to be content with my current circumstances. However, as I mentioned in my story, gratitude is something on which I am working. I must be satisfied with taking Bob's advice and being content to be "secretly incredible." The prophet Micah states, "O man, what is good; and what does the Lord require of you but to love justice, and to love kindness, and to walk humbly with your God?"[363] To me, having traveled the journey of humility that I have, Micah's words seem to be an excellent to-do list. They should also be so for the person you are considering to be your next lead pastor.

Pastor Douglas Hall states, "God does not want us to find a nice way to say what drives us. Rather, He encourages us to confront boldly the real ideas that cause us to take action."[364] I believe that by writing this book I have done that. My desire has been to be helpful to the lay leaders in local churches who have the difficult responsibility of hiring the next pastor to lead their church. While I have tried to say things in a nice way, my larger motive is to boldly confront the issues which I've discussed in regard to the dark side of some pastoral leadership styles, and encourage the transformation which will result through the application of the humility factor. I believe as futurist James Canton states, "We will get the future we create,"[365] so this book is my battle cry for changing the way churches hire their pastors. I want to help create a future in which churches are successful, effective, and healthy because they are led by humble pastors who exhibit not only fantastic leadership qualities and skills, but also all seven of the humility factor attributes. I want to see churches with great leaders who possess humble intelligence.

One of the promptings I had for writing this book was the influence I received from Pastor Graham Standish. Hear his words now.

> So, what is the nature of humble leadership? It is leadership that is radically open to God – in which we lead from faith rather than fear, from willingness to let God's will flow through us rather than willfully insisting that our own will be done, from hope rather than cynicism, from love rather than selfishness, and from God's power rather than our power. If our leaders have humility and a deep openness to God, a conviction that churches are called to follow God, a willingness to be weak so that God's grace and power can flow through us, and a resolute readiness to move people lovingly and compassionately in God's direction, amazing things can happen.[366]

I don't know about you, but I want to hold out for amazing things to happen. I want to see churches become healthy, effective, and successful. I want to see people who love their pastor, their church, and the people of the community that they are serving. I believe it can happen when pastors attain humble intelligence through compassion, sacrificial service, openness, brokenness, self-awareness, forgiveness, and gratitude. I believe that churches can be blessed beyond measure when they have a pastor who exemplifies the humility factor.

ENDNOTES

1   Philippians 2:6-8, English Standard Version.

2   Standish, N. G. (2007). *Humble leadership: Being radically open to God's guidance and grace.* Herndon, VA: The Alban Institute.

3   Edmondson, R. (2015). *10 Attributes of a humble leader.* http://www.ronedmondson.com.

4   Standish. (2007). *Humble leadership.* p. xi.

5   Matthew 22:37-39, ESV.

6   Matthew 28:19-29, ESV.

7   Lewis, C. S. (2001). *Mere Christianity.* San Francisco: Harper. p. 109.

8   Philippians 2:3, ESV.

9   Standish. (2007). *Humble leadership.* p. 4.

10   Bonem, M., & Patterson, R. (2005). *Leading from the second chair: Serving your church, fulfilling your role, and realizing your dreams.* San Francisco: Jossey-Bass. p. 8.

11   Kerfoot, K. (1998). The strategic use of humility. *Nursing Economics,* 16:238-239.

12   Owens, B. P., & Hekman, D. R. (2012). Modeling how to grow: An inductive examination of humble leader behaviors, contingencies, and outcomes. *Academy of Management Journal, 55*(4), 787-818. doi: 10.5465/amj.2010.0441

13   Bright, D. S., Cameron, K. S., & Caza, A. (2006) The amplifying and buffering effects of virtuousness in downsized organizations. *Journal of Business Ethics,* 64: 249-269.

14   Hartwig, R. T., & Bird, W. (2015). *Teams that thrive: Five disciplines of collaborative church leadership.* Downers Grove, IL: IVP Books. p. 170.

15   Hall, D., & Hall, J. (2010). *The cat and the toaster: Living system ministry in a technological age.* Eugene, OR: Wipf & Stock. p. 32.

16   McKeever, J. (2011). *7 tips to finding humility...and keeping it.* http://www.crosswalk.com. p. 20.

17   Atkinson, G. (2010). *Church leadership 101: Stay humble.* http://churchleaders.com. p. 38.

18   Standish. (2007). *Humble leadership.* p. 14.

19   Vooys, J. (1991). No clergy or laity: All Christians are ministers in the body of Christ, Ephesians 4:11-13. *Direction, 20*(1), 87-95.

20   1 Corinthians 3:19, ESV.

21   Owens & Hekman. (2012). *Modeling how to grow.*

22 Pugh, B. (2016). Succession plans: Is there a biblical template? *JEPTA: Journal of the European Pentecostal Theological Association, 36*(2), 117-130. doi: 10.1080/18124461.2016.1184408

23 Standish. (2007). *Humble leadership.*

24 Campolo, T. (1997). *Following Jesus without embarrassing God.* Dallas: WORD Publishing.

25 Hutchison, J. C. (2009). Servanthood: Jesus' countercultural call to Christian leaders. *Bibliotheca sacra, 166*(661), 53-69.

26 Robbins, V. K. (1996). *Exploring the texture of texts: A guide to socio-rhetorical interpretation.* Valley Forge, PA: Trinity Press International.

27 Ferch, S. R. (2015). *Conversations on servant-leadership: Insights on human courage in life and work.* Albany: SUNY Press.

28 Goff, B. (2012). *Love does: Discover a secretly incredible life in an ordinary world.* Nashville, TN: Thomas Nelson. p. 160.

29 Luke 8: 50-56, ESV.

30 Goff. (2012). *Love does.* p. 161.

31 Tripp, D. (2014). *Pastor, are you humble?* http://www.crossway.org.

32 Van Velsor, E., McCauley, C. D., & Ruderman, M. N. (2010). *The center for creative leadership handbook of leadership development* (E. Van Velsor, C. D. McCauley & M. N. Ruderman, Eds. Third ed.). San Francisco: Jossey-Bass.

33 Douglas, S. M. (2014). Developing leaders for pastoral ministry. *The Journal of Applied Christian Leadership, 8*(2), 84-90.

34 Matthew 20:25-27, ESV.

35 Proverbs 16:5, ESV.

36 Sanders, J. O. (2007). *Spiritual leadership: Principles of excellence for every believer.* Chicago: Moody Publishers. p. 155.

37 Kimball, D. (2007). *They like Jesus but not the church: Insights from emerging generations.* Grand Rapids, MI: Zondervan. p. 80.

38 Plastow, J. (2017). *Isn't the Holy Spirit enough?* Regent University.

39 Rokeach, as cited by Ryu, G. (2015). The missing link of value congruence and its consequences. *Public Personnel Management, 44,* 473-495.

40 Vveinhardt, J., Gulbovaite, E. & Streimikiene, D. (2016). Values congruence from the executives' viewpoint. *Value-based Practices. 9,* 248-265.

41 Hitt, M. A., Keats, B. W., Harback, H. F. & Nixon, R. D. (1994). Rightsizing: Building and maintaining strategic leadership and long-term competitiveness. *Organizational Dynamics, 23,* 18-32.

42 Collins, J. (2001). *Good to great: Why some companies make the leap...and others don't,* New York, HarperCollins.

43 Rose, S. C. (1968). Shape and style of the church tomorrow. *Theology Today, 25,* 64-80.

44 Keucher, G. W. (2010). *Humble and strong: Mutually accountable leadership in the church.* Harrisburg, PA: Morehouse Publishing. p. 22.

45 Connelly, S. (2017). *The story of televangelists Jim and Tammy Faye Bakker's fall from grace.* New York Daily News.

46 Shellnutt, K., & Lee, M. (2014). *Mark Driscoll resigns from Mars Hill.* Christianity Today.com.

47 Campolo, T. (1997). *Following Jesus.* p. 271.

48 Bickel, B., & Jantz, S. (1996). *I'm fine with God...it's Christians I can't stand: Getting past the religious garbage in the search for spiritual truth.* Eugene, OR: Harvest House. p. 7.

49 Kimball. (2007). *They like Jesus but not the church.*

50 Ibid., p. 213.

51 http://www.shapingtomorrow.com.

52 http://www.shoebat.com.

53 http://www.Religoustolerance.com.

54 http://www.pewresearchcenter.com.

55 Plastow, J. (2015). *Your pastor might be a narcissist if.* Regent University.

56   Cameron, K. S., & Quinn, R. (2011). *Diagnosing and changing organizational culture: Based on the competing values framework* San Francisco: Jossey-Bass.

57   Kouzes, J. M., & Posner, B. Z. (2012). *The leadership challenge: How to make extraordinary things happen in organizations* (5th ed.). San Francisco, CA: Jossey-Bass. p. 39.

58   Plastow, J. (2015). *Your pastor might be a narcissist if.* Regent University.

59   Standish. (2007). *Humble leadership.*

60   Ibid., p. 2.

61   Keucher. (2010). *Humble and strong.* p. 91.

62   Philippians 2:3, ESV.

63   Canton, J. (2015). *Future smart: Managing the game-changing trends that will transform the world.* Boston: Da Capo Press. p. 93.

64   Chermack, T. J. (2011). *Scenario planning in organizations: How to create, use and assess scenarios.* San Francisco: Berrett-Koehler. p. xv.

65   Hartwig & Bird. (2015). *Teams that thrive.* p. 236.

66   Kimball. (2007). *They like Jesus but not the church.*

67   https://www.acton.org/research/lord-acton-quote-archive.

68   Standish. (2007). *Humble leadership.* p. 10.

69	Van Velsor et al. (2010). *The center for creative leadership.* p. 9.
70	Pascal, B. (1961). *Penses.* London: Penguin Books. p. 64.
71	Keucher. (2010). *Humble and strong.* p. 31.
72	Witherington. (2011). *Work: A kingdom perspective on labor.* p. 35.
73	Isaiah 2:17, ESV.
74	McKeever. (2011). *7 tips to finding humility.* p.22.
75	Ibid.
76	2 Chronicles 34:27, ESV.
77	http://www.pric.org.
78	Chambers, A. (2009). *Eats with sinners: Reaching hungry people like Jesus did.* Cincinnati, OH: Standard Publishing. p. 140.
79	Fedler, K. D. (2006). *Exploring Christian ethics: Biblical foundations for morality.* Louisville, KY: Westminster John Knox Press. p. 88.
80	Oster, G. (2011). *The light prize: Perspectives on Christian innovation.* Virginia Beach, VA: Positive Signs Media. p. 40.
81	Bonem & Patterson. (2005). *Leading from the second chair.* p. xiii.

82 As cited by Plastow, J. (2017). *The art and practices of a potato farmer: What innovators can learn from them.* Regent University.

83 Psalm 25:9, ESV.

84 James 4:20, ESV.

85 Keucher. (2010). *Humble and strong.* p. 15.

86 McElroy, S. E., Rice, K. G., Davis, D. E., Hook, J. N., Hill, P. C., Worthington, E. L., & Van Tongeren, D. R. (2014). Intellectual humility: scale development and theoretical elaborations in the context of religious leadership. *Journal of Psychology & Theology, 42*(1). p. 20.

87 Bekker, C. J. Leading with the head bowed down: Lessons in leadership humility from the rule of St. Benedict of Nursia. *Inner Resources for Leaders.* http://www.regent.edu/acad/global/publications/innerresources/vol1iss3/bekker_inspirational.pdf. p. 2.

88 Ibid., pp. 4-6.

89 Goff. (2012). *Love does.* p. xiv.

90 Hall & Hall. (2010). *The cat and the toaster.* p. 5.

91 Kwakman, H. (2015). A consistent vision of love and compassion. *Compass (10369686), 49*(2), p. 13.

92 Bickel & Jantz. (1996). *I'm fine with God...*p. 180.

93 Campolo. (1997). *Following Jesus*. p. 167.

94 http://www.bible-truth.org/msg100.html.

95 John 11:33-35, ESV.

96 Galatians 6:2, ESV.

97 John 21:15-17, ESV.

98 http://bible-truth.org & John 13:1, ESV.

99 https://www.biblegateway.

100 Hultgren, A. J. (1974). Double commandment of love in Mt. 22:34-40: Its sources and compositions. *The Catholic Biblical Quarterly, 36*(3), 373-378.

101 Laymon, C. M. (1971). *The interpreter's one-volume commentary on the Bible*. New York: Abington Press.

102 http://www.biblehub.com.

103 Matthew 5:43, ESV.

104 Robbins, V. K. (1996). *Exploring the texture of texts: A guide to socio-rhetorical interpretation*. Valley Forge, PA: Trinity Press International.

105 Park, E. C. (2009). A soteriological reading of the great commandment pericope in Matthew 22:34-40. *Biblical Research, 54*, 61-78.

106 1 Corinthians 13:6, ESV.

107 Wright, N. T. (2010). *After you believe: Why Christian character matters.* New York: HarperCollins.

108 Johnston, R., & Finch, A. (2014). Raising hope: Because hope fuels innovation, creativity, and vitality in the church. *Leadership Sum 2014.* p. 210.

109 Schwartz, B. (2012). *Doing the right thing for the right reason.* Retrieved from http://youtube/MkayGd63Rzl.

110 George, B. (2003). *Authentic leadership: Rediscovering the secrets to creating lasting value.* San Francisco: Jossey-Bass. p. 39.

111 Cleveland, C. (2015). Lead like Jesus-really: If you don't have to give up power, then it's not really servant leadership. *Christianity Today, 59*(9), p. 36.

112 Badal, J. (2015). *Four marks of a humble ministry leader.* http://unlockingthebible.org

113 http://www.religion.blogs.cnn.com.

114 Ibid.

115 As cited by Baldoni, J. (2003). *Great communication secrets of great leaders.* New York: McGraw-Hill. p. 143.

116 Matthew 20:28, ESV.

117 John 13:3-5, ESV.

118 Cordeiro, W. (2001). *Doing church as a team*. Ventura, CA: Regal. p. 81.

119 Sinek, S. (2014). *Leaders eat last*. New York: Portfolio/Penguin. p. 66.

120 Goff. (2012). *Love does*. p. 9.

121 Ibid., p. 99.

122 Ibid.

123 Standish. (2007). *Humble leadership*.

124 Matthew 6:1, 3-4, ESV.

125 Scazzero, P. (2017). 10 transformative lessons for healthy churches. *OutreachMagazine.com*.

126 Bornstein, A., & Bornstein, J. (2016). What makes a great leader. *Entrepreneur, 44*(3), 36-45.

127 Nieuwhof, C. (2013). *5 habits that reveal you're a prideful leader: And 5 keys to humility*. https://www.careynieuwhof.com

128 Michalko, M. (2006). *Thinkertoys: A handbook of creative-thinking techniques* (2nd ed.). Berkeley: Ten Speed Press. p. 14.

129 Van Velsor et al. (2010). *The center for creative leadership*.

130 Dess, G. G., & Picken, J. C. (2000). Changing roles: Leadership in the 21st century. *Organizational Dynamics, 28*(3), p. 31.

131 John 3:1-2, ESV.

132 Setran, D. (2016). Conquering the tyrannical commander: Richard Baxter on the perils of pride in Christian ministry. *Christian Education Journal, 13*(1), pp. 64-65.

133 Painter, M. J. (2014). Artificial versus authentic leadership. *T+D, 68*(4), 104-105.

134 Baldoni, J. (2003). *Great communication secrets of great leaders.* New York: McGraw-Hill.

135 Edmondson. (2015). 10 attributes of a humble Leader. http://www.ronedmondson.com. p. 45.

136 Standish. (2007). *Humble leadership.*

137 Edge, R. (2015). From command and control to humble inquiry. *Radiology Management, 37*(6), 48-49.

138 Willis, P. (2016). From humble inquiry to humble intelligence: Confronting wicked problems and augmenting public relations. *Public Relations Review, 42*(2), 306-313. doi: 10.1016/j.pubrev.2015.05.007

139 Proverbs 12:15, ESV.

140 Tokman, E., & Ferguson, K. (2015). Be humble, notice everything, and be fair: A conversation with Orhan Pamuk. *World Literature Today*(6), 9.

141 Plastow, J. (2016). *Crossing borders with humility: A white paper for church leaders*. Regent University.

142 Standish. (2007). *Humble leadership*. p. 137.

143 Scazzero. (2017). *10 transformative lessons for healthy churches*.

144 Matthew 3:16, ESV.

145 Luke 4:1, ESV.

146 Acts 10:38, ESV.

147 Isaiah 42:1, ESV.

148 Romans 8:9, ESV.

149 Mark 14:32-36, ESV.

150 Philippians 2:10-11, ESV.

151 Spielman, L. W. (1999). David's abuse of power. *Word & World, 19*(3), 251-259.

152 James 3:3, ESV.

153 Chamberlin, J. G. (1964). The humble church. *Pittsburgh Perspective, 5*(1), p. 8.

154 Hall & Hall. (2010). *The cat and the toaster.* p. 19.

155 Bonem & Patterson. (2005). *Leading from the second chair.* p. 13.

156 Ibid., p. 23.

157 Lewis. (2001). *Mere Christianity*. p. 114.

158 Collins, J. (2001). *Good to great*. p. 192.

159 Romans 12:1, ESV.

160 Psalm 51:17, ESV.

161 Standish. (2007). *Humble leadership*. p. 33.

162 McArthur-Blair, J. (2010). Fragile practice, humble learning, extraordinary outcomes. *AI Practitioner, 12*(1), p. 8.

163 Plastow. (2016). *Crossing boundaries*.

164 Fedler. (2006). *Exploring Christian ethics* p. 72.

165 As cited by Adams, S. (2008). http://www.christianitytoday.com.

166 1 Peter 1:4, ESV.

167 Mark 9:35, ESV.

168 Mark 10:44, ESV.

169 Philippians 2:6, ESV.

170 Matthew 26:53, ESV.

171 Romans 12:3, ESV.

172   Philippians 2:3, ESV.

173   1 Corinthians 12, ESV.

174   Proverbs 16:18, ESV.

175   Kopelowitz, S. B. (2009). The laws of resonant leadership. *School Administrator, 66*(11), 29-31.

176   Lewis. (2001). *Mere Christianity.* p. 6.

177   Sanders. (2007). *Spiritual leadership.* p. 62.

178   McKeever, J. (2011). *7 tips to finding humility...and keeping it.* http://www.crosswalk.com.

179   Sen, A. (2009). Ego boundaries that cross borders. *International Journal of Business Insights & Transformation, 2*(2), p. 105.

180   Bonem & Patterson. (2005). *Leading from the second chair.* p. 30.

181   Ephesians 1:7, ESV.

182   Psalm 103:12, ESV.

183   Matthew 26:28, ESV.

184   Luke 23:34, ESV.

185   As cited in *Guideposts Magazine.* (August, 2017) Harlan, IA. p. 14.

186 Dierendonck, D., & Patterson, K. (2015). Compassionate love as a cornerstone of servant leadership: An integration of previous theorizing and research. *Journal of Business Ethics, 128*(1), p. 125. doi: 10.1007/s10551-014-2085-z.

187 Ibid.

188 Matthew 6:14-15, ESV.

189 Mark: 11: 25-26, ESV.

190 Luke: 6:37, ESV.

191 Matthew 18:23-35, ESV.

192 Sande, K. (2003). *The peacemaker.* http://www.peacemaker.net/project/true-stories-the-humble-pastor.

193 *Webster's New World Dictionary* (2006). Cleveland, OH: Wiley Publishing, Inc.

194 Edmondson (2015). *10 attributes.* p. 45.

195 Psalm 136:1, ESV.

196 Dierendonck & Patterson. (2015). *Compassionate love.* p. 125.

197 1 Thessalonians 5:18, ESV.

198 Matthew 23:6, ESV.

199 Colossians 3:17, ESV.

200 Psalm 9:1, ESV.

201 As cited by Behary, W. T. (2013). *Disarming the narcissist: Surviving & thriving with the self-absorbed.* Oakland, CA: New Harbinger Publications, Inc. p. 85.

202 Witherington III, B. (2011). *Work: A kingdom perspective on labor.* Grand Rapids, MI: William B. Eerdmans Publishing Company. p. 15.

203 Bornstein, A., & Bornstein, J. (2016). What makes a great leader. *Entrepreneur, 44*(3), 36-45.

204 Bonem & Patterson. (2005). *Leading from the second chair.* p. 19.

205 Fuda, P., & Winn, B. A. (2017). Change champs and change chumps: A story of leaders, burning ambition, and alignment. *People & Strategy, 40*(2), 58-62.

206 Standish. (2007). *Humble leadership.* p. 13.

207 Sinek. (2014). *Leaders eat last.* pp. 67-68.

208 2 Corinthians 4:7, ESV.

209 Bonem & Patterson. (2005). *Leading from the second chair.* p. 27.

210 Kinnison, Q. P. (2014). The pastor as expert and the challenge of being a saltwater fish in a freshwater tank. *Journal of Religious Leadership, 13*(1), p.2.

211 http://www.recklesslyalive.com/12-reasons-millennials-are-over-church.

212 Croft, B. (2015). *The pastor's ministry: Biblical priorities for faithful shepherds.* Grand Rapids, MI: Zondervan. p. 37

213 http://www.learn.org.

214 http://ronedmondson.com.

215 http://www.acts29.com/biblical-qualifications-of-a-pastor.

216 http://www.my-pastor.com.

217 http://www.frtommylane.com.

218 Hersey, P. (1985). The situational leader. New York: Warner. (as cited by Owens & Hekman, p. 789).

219 Greenleaf, R. K. (1996). *On becoming a servant leader* (D. M. Frick, Spears, L. C., Ed.). San Francisco: Jossey-Bass. p. 25.

220 1 Peter 5:5, ESV.

221 Sanders. (2007). *Spiritual leadership.* p. 49.

222 Owens & Hekman. (2012). *Modeling how to grow.* p. 787.

223 Keucher. (2010). *Humble and strong.* p. 1, 36.

224 Nouwen, H. (1992). *In the name of Jesus: Reflections on Christian leadership.* New York: Crossroad Publishing Company.

225 Ibid., p. 79.

226 http://www.babylonbee.com/news/megachurch-stage-collapses-pastors-massive-ego.

227 Bekker, C. J. (n.d.). Leading with the head bowed down: Lessons in leadership humility from the rule of St. Benedict of Nursia. *Inner Resources for Leaders.* http://www.regent.edu/acad/global/ publications/innerresources/vol1iss3/bekker_inspirational.pdf.

228 Bonem & Patterson. (2005). *Leading from the second chair.*

229 Collins, J. (2001). *Good to great: Why some companies make the leap...and others don't.* New York: HarperCollins.

230 Spielman. (1999). *David's abuse of power.*

231 Joosten, A., Dijke, M., Hiel, A., & Cremer, D. (2014). Being "in control" may make you lose control: The role of self-regulation in unethical leadership behavior. *Journal of Business Ethics, 121*(1), 1-14. doi: 10.1007/s10551-013-1686-2

232 Ludwig, D. C., & Longenecker, C. O. (1993). The Bathsheba syndrome: The ethical failure of successful leaders. *Journal of Business Ethics, 12*(4), 265-273.

233 Ibid., pp. 265, 267.

234 McSwain, S. (2013). *Why nobody wants to go to church anymore.* http://www.huffingtonpost.com.

235   Greenleaf, R. (1977). *Servant leadership: A journey into the nature of legitimate power and greatness.* New York: Paulist. p. 104.

236   Azanza, G., Moriano, J. A., & Molero, F. (2013). Authentic leadership and organizational culture as drivers of employees' job satisfaction. *Liderazgo auténtico y cultura organizacional como impulsores de la satisfacción laboral de los trabajadores (Spanish; Castilian), 29*, 45-50. doi: 10.5093/tr2013a7

237   Fusco, T., O'Riordan, S., & Palmer, S. (2015). Authentic leaders are... conscious, competent, confident, and congruent: A grounded theory of group coaching and authentic leadership development. *International Coaching Psychology Review, 10*(2), p. 132.

238   Walumbwa, F. O., Christensen, A. L., & Hailey, F. (2011). Authentic leadership and the knowledge economy: Sustaining motivation and trust among knowledge workers. *Organizational Dynamics, 40*, 110-118. doi: 10.1016/j.orgdyn.2011.01.005

239   Olson, E. E., & Eoyang, G. H. (2001). *Facilitating organization change: Lessons from complexity science.* San Francisco: Jossey-Bass/Pfieffer.

240   Kimball. (2007). *They like Jesus but not the church.* p. 80.

241   Weidner, C. K., II, & Purohit, Y. S. (2009). When power has leaders: Some indicators of power-addiction among

organizational leaders. *Journal of Organizational Culture, Communications and Conflict,* (1), 83.

242 Garner, J. T. (2012). Uncomfortable communication: Leaders' and members' perceptions of dissent triggers in churches. *Journal of Communication & Religion, 35*(1), 50-72.

243 Losey, M., Meisinger, S., & Ulrich, D. (2005). *The future of human resource management: 64 thought leaders explore the critical HR issues of today and tomorrow* (M. Losey, S. Meisinger & D. Ulrich, Eds.). Hoboken, NJ: John Wiley & Sons.

244 Lewis. (2001). *Mere Christianity.* pp. 110, 112.

245 1 Peter 5:3, ESV.

246 De Hoogh, A. H. B., Greer, L. L., & Den Hartog, D. N. (2015). Diabolical dictators or capable commanders? An investigation of the differential effects of autocratic leadership on team performance. *The Leadership Quarterly, 26,* 687-701. doi: 10.1016/j.leaqua.2015.01.001

247 Burke, W. W. (2014). *Organization change: Theory and practice.* Los Angeles: SAGE.

248 Keucher. (2010). *Humble and strong.*

249 Ibid., p.10.

250   Sen, A. (2009). Ego boundaries that cross borders. *International Journal of Business Insights & Transformation, 2*(2), 104-108.

251   Plastow. (2016). *Crossing borders.*

252   Kwakman, H. (2015). A consistent vision of love and compassion. *Compass (10369686), 49*(2), 10-14.

253   Standish, N. G. (2007). Whatever happened to humility? Rediscovering a misunderstood leadership strength. *Congregations, 33*(2), 22-26.

254   Plastow. (2016). *Crossing borders.*

255   Bonem & Patterson. (2005). *Leading from the second chair.*

256   Greiner, L. (1998). Evolution and revolution as organizations grow. *Harvard Business Review,* May-June, 55-67.

257   Chambers. (2009). *Eats with sinners.*

258   Ibid., p. 144.

259   Standish. (2007). *Humble leadership.* p. 17.

260   As cited by Chambers. (2009). *Eats with sinners.* p. 150.

261   Dowbiggin, I. A. N. (2015). The Americanization of narcissism. *American Historical Review, 120*(2), 562.

262 Behary, W. T. (2013). *Disarming the narcissist: Surviving & thriving with the self-absorbed.* Oakland, CA: New Harbinger Publications, Inc. p. 13.

263 Standish. (2007). *Humble leadership.*

264 Fedler, K. D. (2006). *Exploring Christian ethics: Biblical foundations for morality.* Louisville, KY: Westminster John Knox Press.

265 Newton, N., Herr, J., Pollack, J., & McAdams, D. (2014). Selfless or selfish? Generativity and narcissism as components of legacy. *Journal of Adult Development, 21*(1), 59-68. doi: 10.1007/s10804-013-9179-1

266 Behary, W. T. (2013). *Disarming the narcissist.* p. 13.

267 Sanders, J. O. (2007). *Spiritual leadership.*

268 Hackman, M. Z., & Johnson, C. E. (2013). *Leadership: A communication perspective* (6th Ed.). Long Grove, IL: Waveland Press, Inc.

269 Erickson, A., Shaw, B., Murray, J., & Branch, S. (2015). Destructive leadership: Causes, consequences and countermeasures. *Organizational Dynamics, 44,* 266-272. doi: 10.1016/j.orgdyn.2015.09.003

270 Sankowsky, D. (1995). The charismatic leader as narcissist: Understanding the abuse of power. *Organizational Dynamics, 23*(4), 57-71.

271 Unknown author. (2013). When your pastor speaks humility, but shows pride instead. htttps://www.spiritualsoundingboard.com.

272 Obadiah 1:3, ESV.

273 Plastow, J. (2015). *Your pastor might be a narcissist.* p. 3.

274 Engstrom, T. W. (1976). *The making of a Christian leader.* Grand Rapids, MI: Zondervan Pub. House.

275 htttps://www.spiritualsoundingboard.com.

276 Plastow, J. (2015). *Your pastor might be a narcissist.* p. 2.

277 Goleman, D., Boyatzis, R., & McKee, A. (2013). *Primal leadership: Unleashing the power of emotional intelligence* (Tenth anniversary ed.). Boston, MA: Harvard Business Review Press. p. 72.

278 Ibid.

279 Keucher. (2010). *Humble and strong.*

280 Nieuwhof, C. (2014). *5 reasons people have stopped attending your church (especially Millennials).* http://www.careynieuwhof.com.

281 Goudzwaard, B., Vander Vennen, M., & Van Heemst, D. (2007). *Hope in troubled times: A new vision for confronting global crisis.* Grand Rapids, MI: Baker Academic.

282 Bickel & Jantz. (1996). *I'm fine with God.* pp. 15-16.

283 Matthew 23:4, ESV.

284 Setran. (2016). *Conquering the tyrannical commander.*

285 Goudzwaard et al. (2007). *Hope in troubled times.* p. 29.

286 Boyatzis, R., & McKee, A. (2006). Inspiring others through resonant leadership. *Business Strategy Review, 17*(2), 15-19. doi: 10.1111/j.0955-6419.2006.00394.x

287 Kopelowitz, S. B. (2009). The laws of resonant leadership. *School Administrator, 66*(11), 29-31.

288 Watson, R. (2014). 21st century management: Resonant leadership and emotional intelligence. *ACA News (American Chiropractic Association), 10*(7), p. 36.

289 Plastow, J. (2014). *All things leadership: Real life practices from the trenches of leadership.* Greeley, CO: Xulon Press.

290 Greenleaf. (1977). *Servant leadership.*

291 Dierendonck & Patterson. (2015). Compassionate love.

292 Ayers, M. (2006). Toward a theology of leadership. *Journal of Biblical Perspectives in Leadership, 1*(1), 18.

293 1 Corinthians 12, ESV.

294 Philippians 2:3, ESV.

295 Faulkner, R. (2010). Honorable ambition: Reply to critics. *Perspectives on Political Science, 39*(4), 202.

296 Standish. (2007). *Humble leadership*. p. 17.

297 Nouwen. (1992). *In the name of Jesus*. p. 62.

298 Rothwell, W. J., Stavros, J. M., & Sullivan, R. L. (2016). *Practicing organization development: Leading transformation and change*. Hoboken, NJ: Wiley.

299 Raj, R., & Srivastava, K. B. L. (2016). Transformational leadership and innovativeness: The mediating role of organizational learning. *Journal of Management Research (09725814), 16*(4), 201-219.

300 Standish. (2007). *Humble leadership*. p. 11.

301 Raj & Srivastava. (2016). *Transformational leadership*. p. 201.

302 Rothwell et al. (2016). *Practicing organizational development*. p. 79.

303 Kornusky, J. R. M., & Heering, H. R. C. (2017). *Leadership and motivation*. Ipswich, MA: EBSCO Publishing.

304 Sang Long, C., Chin Fei, G., Adam, M. B. H., & Owee Kowang, T. (2016). Transformational leadership, empowerment, and job satisfaction: The mediating role of employee empowerment. *Human Resources for Health, 14*, 1-14. doi: 10.1186/s12960-016-0171-2

305 Barrett, M. (2015). The duty of a pastor: John Owen on feeding the flock by diligent preaching of the word. *Themelios, 40*(3), 459-472.

306 Matthew 3:2, ESV.

307 Rothwell et al. (2016). Practicing organizational development. p. 401.

308 Lewis. (2001). *Mere Christianity*.

309 Bommarito, N. (2014). Patience and perspective. *Philosophy East & West, 64*(2), 269-286.

310 Psalm 106:13, ESV.

311 1 Samuel 8-9, ESV.

312 Proverbs 27:23, ESV.

313 Colossians 3:12, ESV.

314 Proverbs 15:22, ESV.

315 Proverbs 19:20, ESV.

316 Morag, O., & Barakonyi, K. (2010). Business at the speed of light - The role of time and speed on business strategy. *Vezetéstudomány / Budapest Management Review, 41*(6), 36-39.

317 Leading people through change: How to manage your most valuable asset. (2007). *Strategic Direction, 23*(5), 20-23.

318 Plastow, J. (2017). *Due diligence in a 140-character world*. Regent University.

319 Grady, J. L. (2016). *How a humble African pastor rocked my world.* http://www.charismanews.com/opinion/60515-how-a-humble-african-pastor-rocked-my-world

320 2 Corinthians 12, ESV.

321 Hall & Hall. (2010). *The cat and the toaster.*

322 Burke, W. W. (2014). *Organization change: Theory and practice.* Los Angeles: SAGE.

323 Unknown Author. (1995) Hiring a pastor 1995-style. *The Christian Century.* p. 954.

324 Isaiah 66:2, ESV.

325 Losey et al. (2005). *The future of human resource management.* p. 69.

326 Keucher. (2010). *Humble and strong.*

327 Perry, T. (2017). *Toxic leadership: 5 people churches should never hire.* Echurch. p. 5.

328 As cited by McLaren, B. D., Stevens, B., Moss, O., Yamasaki, A., Watkins, A. J., Merritt, C. H., & Hill, B. N. (2014). Books for ministry: Seven pastors pick the 21st-century works they've found most helpful. *The Christian Century, 131*(21), 30.

329 Standish. (2007). *Humble leadership.* p. 16.

330 Sanders. (2007). *Spiritual leadership.* p. 62.

331 Psalm 25:9, ESV.

332 Douglas, S. M. (2014). Developing leaders for pastoral ministry. *The Journal of Applied Christian Leadership, 8*(2), 84-90.

333 Vicere, A. A. (2004). *Coaching and mentoring: Best advice for leaders: Stop, look and listen.* https://www.leader-values.com/article.php?aid=109.

334 Zheng, W., & Muir, D. (2015). Embracing leadership: A multifaceted model of leader identity development. *Leadership & Organization Development Journal, 36*(6), 630.

335 Dess, G. G., & Picken, J. C. (2000). Changing roles: Leadership in the 21st century. *Organizational Dynamics, 28*(3), 19.

336 Pugh. (2016). *Succession plans.*

337 Acts 13:22, ESV.

338 1 Chronicles 28:6, ESV.

339 1 Corinthians 3:19, ESV.

340 Hartwig & Bird. (2015). *Teams that thrive.* p. 160.

341 Pugh. (2016). *Succession plans.*

342 Standish. (2007). *Humble leadership.*

343 Stanley, A. (2006). *Catalyst session one.* https://www.catalystleader.com/read/andy-stanley-session-1.

344 McKnight, W. (2010). *90 days to success in consulting.* Boston: COURSE TECHNOLOGY: CENGAGE Learning. p. 221.

345 Owens & Hekman. *(2012). Modeling how to grow.*

346 Sanders. (2007). *Spiritual leadership.*

347 Hartwig & Bird. (2015). *Teams that thrive.* p. 169.

348 Kimball. (2007). *They like Jesus.* p. 32.

349 Bickel & Jantz. (1996). *I'm fine with God.*

350 Berkun, S. (2010). *The myths of innovation.* Sebastopol, CA: O'Reilly. p. 40.

351 Plastow, J. (2016). *The other half.* http://www.johnplastow.com/all-things-leadership.

352 Cordeiro, W. (2001). *Doing church as a team.* Ventura, CA: Regal. pp. 58-60.

353 Bonem & Patterson. (2005). *Leading from the second chair.*

354 Proverbs 6:17, ESV.

355 http://www.charismanews.com

356 McKeever. (2011). *7 tips to finding humility.* p.23.

357 https://www.pri.org/stories/2017-05-01/biggest-megachurch-earth-facing-crisis-evangelism

358   Proverbs 24:4, ESV.

359   Rainer, T. S. (2014). *Humility and the Christian leader.* http://www.lifeway.com.

360   Chismar, J. (2009). *12 ways to humble yourself.* https://www.billygraham.org.

361   As cited by Chambers. (2017). *Eats with sinners.* p. 150.

362   Goff. (2012). *Love does.* p. 163.

363   Micah 6:8, ESV.

364   Hall & Hall. (2010). *The cat and the toaster.* pp. 10-11.

365   Canton. (2015). *Future smart.* p. xiv.

366   Standish. (2007). *Humble leadership.* pp. 22 & 26.

About the Author

Dr. John Plastow

John serves as an executive coach, church leadership advisor, and strategic and creative consultant. He holds a doctorate in strategic leadership from Regent University and a master's degree in organizational management with a specialization in leadership. He is a published writer for academic journals, the popular press, and gospel music publishers. He serves as an adjunct online professor for multiple universities, a workshop leader and conference presenter, and has been a full-time pastor for 25 years.

His blog is featured at johnplastow.com. He can be contacted at jrplastow@gmail.com, www.facebook.com/johnrplastow, and https://www.linkedin.com/in/johnplastow. He has been married to Karen since college and they have three terrific children, John II, Melody, and Heather.

Join Us at humblepastors.net

This website is designed specifically to encourage pastors, church leaders, and congregation members to share their experiences in regards to pastors of churches who have shown the seven qualities outlined in *The Humility Factor* and are serving with humble intelligence. In this forum you can tell a story of your pastor or a pastor you know who is demonstrating the humble service that Jesus modeled. It is our hope that together we will create a library of the stories of pastors who truly minister with humility in service to the Lord Jesus and His church.

You will also have the opportunity to benefit from posts, papers, and more as I continue to study the many facets of church leadership, pastoral challenges, administrative issues, staff and leadership relationships, and, of course, how to be a pastor of humble intelligence. There is a link to johnplastow.com, which is the home for John's blog, All Things Leadership, and a place where you can ask him questions. Finally, with your email registration, you can opt in for downloads of *The Humility Factor* leadership assessment and other valuable tools.

We hope that you will visit humblepastors.net and that you find it to be a valuable, inspiring, and encouraging place to spend a little time. Come back often as new stories and materials will continue to be added.

John Can Help You and Your Church Put *The Humility Factor* into Action

Is your church in the process of hiring a new lead pastor?

With his newly-released book, *The Humility Factor,* as a guide, John will help you navigate the entire process of evaluation of the needs and requirements specific to your unique church and circumstances, recruitment of quality candidates, and what to look for in the interviewing process relating to pastoral leadership styles and evidence of humble intelligence as modeled by Jesus. John will work alongside your board, search committee, and hiring team from the beginning of the pastoral search through the installation of your new pastor.

Order John's Other Recent Book

ALL THINGS LEADERSHIP: Real Life Practices from the Trenches of Leadership

ALL THINGS LEADERSHIP: Real Life Practices from the Trenches of Leadership is a comprehensive treasury of leadership lessons told through John Plastow's unique lens of personal experience, humor, and the high-energy, enthusiastic approach he's used in leading thousands of people during his career. This book will motivate and encourage leaders to raise their standards, expand their vision, give their best, and above all, serve the people entrusted to them. It will also help leaders achieve great things beyond their wildest dreams!

www.johnplastow.com

Made in the USA
San Bernardino, CA
22 February 2018